W0114393

THE ESSENCE OF MUAY THAI

THE ESSENCE OF
MUAY THAI

A Warrior's Guide to the Tradition and Its Spiritual Heart

Nuakai Aru

SHAMBHALA

Shambhala Publications, Inc.
2129 13th Street
Boulder, Colorado 80302
www.shambhala.com

Copyright © 2025 by Nuakai Aru

Cover art: Illustration by Phil Harvey. Pattern by Folksterno/Shutterstock
Cover design: Daniel Urban-Brown
Interior design: Anna Becker

All rights reserved. No part of this book may be reproduced in any form or by
any means, electronic or mechanical, including photocopying, recording, or
by any information storage and retrieval system, without permission in
writing from the publisher.

9 8 7 6 5 4 3 2 1

FIRST EDITION
Printed in the United States of America

Shambhala Publications makes every effort to print on acid-free,
recycled paper. Shambhala Publications is distributed worldwide by
Penguin Random House, Inc., and its subsidiaries.

LIBRARY OF CONGRESS CATALOGING-IN-PUBLICATION DATA
Names: Aru, Nuakai, author.
Title: The essence of Muay Thai: a warrior's guide to the tradition
and its spiritual heart / Nuakai Aru.
Other titles: Warrior's guide to the tradition and its spiritual heart
Description: First edition. | Boulder, Colorado: Shambhala, [2025]
Identifiers: LCCN 2025003515 | ISBN 9781645473817 (trade paperback)
Subjects: LCSH: Muay Thai. | Kickboxing—Thailand. |
Martial arts—Religious aspects.
Classification: LCC GV1127.T45 A78 2025 | DDC 796.815—dc23/eng/20250325
LC record available at https://lccn.loc.gov/2025003515

The authorized representative in the EU for product safety
and compliance is eucomply OÜ, Pärnu mnt 139b-14, 11317 Tallinn, Estonia,
hello@eucompliancepartner.com.

CONTENTS

THE ESSENCE OF MUAY THAI

INTRODUCTION

In the martial arts world, Thailand is the birthplace of Muay Thai, the art and science of "eight limbs," broadly known internationally as Thai boxing. Its ancient roots are a renowned combat system known today as Muay Boran, which developed as a protective tool for the Siamese people of Southeast Asia. Muay Boran encompassed diverse regional styles and effectively integrated hand-to-hand combat with weapons such as swords, shields, and spears.

In the modern era, Muay Thai has achieved global recognition through its exposure on prestigious platforms like mixed martial arts (MMA), K1, and the Ultimate Fighter Competition (UFC). These arenas have become melting pots where fighters from diverse disciplines such as wrestling, boxing, Brazilian jiujitsu, judo, taekwondo, capoeira, sambo, and Muay Thai clash to test their skills and styles. As the sport evolved, blending various techniques became crucial for success inside the cage. Among these disciplines, Brazilian jiujitsu, wrestling, traditional boxing, and Muay Thai have emerged as the most practical and influential, producing numerous champions and shaping the landscape of contemporary combat sports.

I have practiced Muay Thai since the age of sixteen, initially drawn by its demands for physical fitness, skill, and discipline. Over years of dedicated training, I also immersed myself in the art's rich history, intricate techniques, and spiritual dimension.

What began as a physical pursuit evolved into a profound journey of personal growth and self-discovery. Muay Thai became a way of life grounded in teachings of resilience, respect, and spiritual insight that continues to shape my path forward. I completed many training camps in the UK and Thailand and fought briefly as an amateur, although I was unable to continue due to injuries. Instead, I dedicated my martial arts journey to self-healing and personal development. I have now practiced Muay Thai for nearly three decades and taught it for two.

Often taking up a martial art begins out of fear and a hunger to protect oneself or others. This mirrors the origins of Muay Thai, which was developed in ancient Siam by local people seeking self-defense, liberation from oppression, and a path of spiritual guidance. While Muay Thai is often practiced as a fighting sport, its rich history and culture are deeply intertwined with Thailand's past and can also serve as a path of spiritual and personal growth. While at first glance it might appear to be just another aggressive and sometimes brutal fighting style, in reality this art is rooted in the ideals of justice and safeguarding others.

Muay Thai emerged in the modern era as a refined sport omitting the lethal techniques of warfare, focusing instead on competitive prowess and physical conditioning. It engages the eight limbs of two hands, two elbows, two knees, and two legs. In Muay Boran, the head represented a ninth weapon, employed for delivering headbutts, but in both arts, the head represents strategy and tactical thinking. As a fighting system, Muay Thai is more comparable to the game of chess rather than checkers. Elite Muay Thai fighters compete in intense battles of mind, body, and spirit.

Muay Thai has become a highly effective fighting system, celebrated not only for its physical prowess but also for its profound rituals and traditions. Ceremonies such as the Wai Khru (paying respect to one's teachers) and the Ram Muay (a ceremonial war dance) are integral to its practice, emphasizing respect, honor, discipline, and a connection to the fighter's heritage. Beneath its explosive techniques and disciplined training is a lesser-known, esoteric side infused with spiritual dimensions that elevate Muay Thai beyond mere physical combat.

Muay Thai draws deeply from Thailand's mythological and spiritual fabric, weaving together influences from ancient Hindu epics, animist traditions, and Buddhist teachings, reflecting stories of cosmic battles between gods, humans, animals, and demons, embedding within the martial art a sense of divine purpose, spiritual warfare, and a connection to universal forces. This blend of myth, spirituality, and physical mastery enriches the practice, offering fighters a path of personal transformation rooted in both physical skill and spiritual depth.

In *The Essence of Muay Thai*, I draw from my many years of training in Muay Thai and studying martial arts; my life experiences; and my work as a martial arts teacher, well-being coach, educator, filmmaker, and actor to share with you insights on history, cultural heritage, spiritual consciousness, and social empowerment of Muay Thai. Martial arts has been a lifelong journey of personal development, guiding me to physical, emotional, mental, and spiritual growth. Muay Thai specifically has been more than a martial art for me, it has given me the strength of character to investigate the unknown, overcome my limitations, and stand up with confidence to live a life of meaning and purpose.

The Essence of Muay Thai invites you into the enigmatic world of Thai martial arts, weaving together ancient history, spiritual mythology, and martial ethics with practical insights into combat and personal development. It is a journey beyond the physical techniques to the mystical realms of spiritual and physical warfare, magical talismans, sacred rituals, and the wisdom of hermit sages. It unveils a warrior's noble path of hard training, sacrifice, personal transformation, and disciplined introspection. Let every breath, every page, and every story take you on a journey of martial mastery.

CHAPTER ONE

THE ORIGINS OF THAILAND'S HISTORY

THE AWAKENING OF A WARRIOR

It was late on a Saturday evening, almost bedtime. I had gone to stay with my Jamaican dad in Enfield, London, that weekend. The room was dimly lit, with only the flicker of the TV screen cutting through the darkness and casting long shadows. My father had allowed me to stay up late to watch a new martial arts film called *Bloodsport*. The movie features Jean-Claude Van Damme as an American soldier who goes AWOL to compete in an illegal martial arts tournament in Hong Kong. The film showcased diverse martial arts including ninjutsu, karate, taekwondo, kung fu, Brazilian jiujitsu, sumo wrestling, boxing, and Muay Thai, each used by fighters from different ethnicities and backgrounds.

I was only seven years old, but I was captivated by the fluid dance of combat—the seamless blocks, evasions, and strikes of the martial artists. Yet even more than the fighting itself, what truly inspired me was the personal transformation. It was how this intense training could mold a young boy, someone who knew so little, into a mature man—a deadly, yet respectful master of the art. It was more than entertainment: it was a call to something dormant within me, a resonant voice whispering of skill, strength, discipline, and self-control. Every fluid movement struck a chord within me. The sheer displays of willpower resonated deep in my core. I was completely enthralled, and that night a seed was planted in my young heart that would later grow into a relentless pursuit.

Being of Jamaican and British heritage, I also felt a profound connection to the diverse array of fighters portrayed in the film. My Jamaican father had a serious demeanor but could be playful, whereas my British mother appeared playful but had a serious side. Both possessed unique skills and capabilities, and I gleaned a multitude of valuable lessons and advantages from my experiences with both of them. Their eight-year-long relationship marked by differences in culture, upbringing, and personal needs ultimately couldn't withstand the evolving challenges they faced. My father's desire for independence and infidelity clashed with my mother's need for security and her own quest for independence, all while she dealt with health issues—particularly her struggle with arthritis. Perhaps with better support and communication, they might have learned to overcome their challenges. However, when I was just four years old, my mother decided to leave my father. And in spite of his wish for reconciliation, my father respected her choice, and they eventually developed a courteous friendship.

My interest in martial arts did not fade when I returned to my mother's house that Sunday in the small village of Harlington, Bedfordshire, about an hour outside of London. I couldn't help but try out flying kicks all around the place. "What's gotten into him?" my mum asked, casting a disapproving glance at my dad. "The boy's into martial arts," he replied.

And so, at the age of seven, I began to get into the dynamic world of kickboxing and the intricate techniques of Japanese jujitsu. I was instantly hooked. The intensity of the training, the excitement of gaining new moves, the joy of overcoming each challenge, the freedom of learning, and the camaraderie of fellow young warriors became my world.

Unfortunately, my newfound passion was short-lived. Within a year, as my mother focused more intently on her career and aspired for me to receive a top-class education, I was dispatched to a boarding school, and my martial arts journey came to an abrupt halt.

Southeast Asia and the Roots of a Nation

The origins of Muay Boran and Muay Thai are shrouded in legend and myth, and few historical records exist. However, in this chapter, I will share what is known.

The precise origins and age of Thai martial arts remain uncertain, but many assert that the precursor of Muay Thai, Muay Boran, is more than two thousand years old. According to the Institute of the Art of Muay Thai and the Department of Physical Education at the National Stadium of Thailand, the earliest references to Muay Thai can be traced back to 657 C.E., during the Haripuñjaya period, which saw the establishment of a school of liberal and martial arts by a hermit named Sukatanta. The Haripuñjaya Kingdom, located in what is now northern Thailand around modern-day Lamphun, was founded by the Mon people in the seventh century. The Mon people played a significant role in shaping the culture, religion, and martial traditions of the region, including the early forms of unarmed combat that would eventually evolve into Muay, meaning movement, boxing, or fighting. These ancient fighting systems were clearly developed and documented during the rise of the Suk-hothai kingdom in the thirteenth through fourteenth centuries. They were later refined and expanded during the Ayutthaya period in the fourteenth through eighteenth centuries, when warriors used Muay as a means to defend their nation.

However, to truly comprehend the martial arts of Southeast Asia, we need to explore the diverse people, cultures, kingdoms, and empires of the region that have all contributed to this rich heritage over the generations. The peopling of Southeast Asia in ancient times involved multiple waves of migration and the intermingling of diverse ethnic groups over thousands of years.

The initial inhabitants of Southeast Asia are believed to be the Negrito tribes, a population with a history that traces back over twenty-five thousand years as the direct descendants of some of the first humans to leave Africa. This diverse and resilient group established their communities across an area encompassing regions of Cambodia, Thailand, Laos, the Malay Peninsula, the Andaman Islands, the Philippines, and other isolated locales within Asia and Southeast Asia. Often characterized by their shorter stature, darker skin, and black curly hair, the Negritos primarily adopted a hunter-gatherer lifestyle, a testament to their intimate connection with the natural environment and adaptability. There are still Negrito populations residing across Southeast Asia, like the Aeta in the Philippines, the Semang in Malaysia, the Andamanese in the Andaman Islands, and the Mani in Thailand.

In Thailand, the Mani, historically and to some extent currently, live a seminomadic lifestyle in tune with nature, sustaining themselves through hunting, gathering, and fishing. They were adept at slash-and-burn farming, cultivating staples like yams and taro, and their spiritual life was deeply entwined with their environment. They revered the spirits residing in the natural world around them—in the towering trees, the rushing rivers, and the majestic mountains. For the Mani people, as with many other indigenous tribes, animism intertwined with their daily lives and cultural practices. Their spiritual beliefs typically involve a deep respect for nature and the idea that spirits play an active role in their lives. Their animistic rituals included ceremonies and practices aimed at appeasing or communicating with these spirits, which are thought to influence various aspects of the natural world and human life. Their craftsmanship, a reflection of their profound bond with the forest, is evident in the tools and utensils they expertly crafted from natural materials.

Since these earliest groups first came to the area, various tribes and cultures have migrated into and across Southeast Asia, influencing the people and cultures existing there. The ancestors of the Mon and the Khmer peoples, part of the Austroasiatic language family, are believed to have migrated into the region around four thousand to five thousand years ago. Their descendants much later developed the Mon and Khmer civilizations. The Khmer Empire grew into one of the most renowned and far-reaching powers among the early Southeast Asian civilizations. Founded by the self-declared god King Jayavarman II, it spanned around six hundred years, from about 800 to the 1400s. Jayavarman II's ascension to power around 802 marked an era that would witness the rise of a formidable and culturally vibrant civilization centered in what is modern-day Cambodia. From the onset, the Khmer Empire was deeply rooted in Hindu religious traditions mixed with local spiritual beliefs. Jayavarman II proclaimed himself a universal monarch or *chakravartin* and a godking or *devaraja*, making him the incarnation of Shiva, the Hindu god, or his divine representative on earth, which acted not just as a religious tenet but also a political tool to reinforce his authority.

This empire under Jayavarman II's leadership extended its influence far beyond its core territory, exerting control and impact over a significant part of Southeast Asia including present-day Cambodia, parts of Laos, Thailand, Vietnam, Myanmar, and Malaysia. It was a period characterized by remarkable architectural achievements, sophisticated water distribution structures, and a merging of art, religion, and culture that profoundly shaped the societies and cultures within its realm.

The empire was organized in a feudal manner. Land and people were controlled by the nobility, who in turn owed allegiance to the king. This system allowed the king to assemble the resources and labor essential for large construction projects, including temples and water management systems. The empire was renowned not only for its political, trading, and military might but also as a hub for spiritual exploration and expression. Rooted in Hinduism, it wove a unified tapestry of faith where the cosmic dances of Shiva and the benevolent grace of Vishnu were fervently celebrated. A pinnacle of this spiritual development was the religious and political center of Angkor Wat. This temple complex, initially dedicated to Vishnu, remains an architectural marvel, showcasing intricate carvings of the people, culture, and celestial alignments attesting to the empire's grandeur and profound religious devotion. Its masterful carvings vividly portray scenes of people engaged in combat, demonstrating postures and techniques that suggest a sophisticated fighting system. This imagery provides the oldest tangible visual record of the ancient martial arts used in the region.

Kbach Kun Khmer Boran is the umbrella term that encompasses all traditional Khmer martial arts. It represents ancient techniques and fighting methods passed down through generations, featuring a wide array of strategies historically used in combat and self-defense. This includes the techniques of Bokator—encompassing strikes, kicks, joint locks, throws, and ground fighting—as well as the dynamic striking style of Kun

Khmer, known for its powerful kicks, punches, elbows, and knee strikes. These ancient fighting systems were closely linked to the military and served as essential training tools shaping the combat skills and strategic prowess of soldiers. Together, these arts encompass over one thousand years of rich history and cultural heritage.

The Khmer Empire's strategic location enabled a widespread trade network connecting it with China, India, and the Indonesian archipelago. This network facilitated the exchange of goods like agricultural products, metals, and ceramics and fostered cultural exchanges, reinforcing the empire's status as a significant economic and cultural player in the region. As time went on new waves of people continued to migrate into and out of Southeast Asia along these established routes bringing with them unique customs, new languages, trade goods, and traditions, making the living mosaic of people and cultures across the region we know today.

In the period between 800 and 1200, the Tai people steadily migrated from their ancestral lands in modern-day southern China and eventually settled in the lush, tropical regions of modern-day Thailand, Laos, and Cambodia. They were driven by political pressures, the quest for arable lands, and escaping the conflicts of various Chinese dynasties. The land they encountered was a place of abundant natural beauty teeming with wildlife and home to diverse cultures. The Tai people called this land Siam, and over time, they established thriving communities, built impressive temples, and as communities mixed, developed their own unique culture and traditions.

Meanwhile, in the area known today as Cambodia, the spiritual journey of the Khmer Empire was not static. While the Khmer Empire is often remembered for its architectural marvels and grand temples, its spiritual evolution was equally dynamic. Hinduism was the dominant faith of the empire, which gradually gave way to the influence of Mahayana Buddhism. This was not an abrupt transition; it was a gradual process shaped by trade, diplomacy, and evolving cultural ideals. Mahayana Buddhism spread into the Khmer region primarily through maritime trade routes connecting Southeast Asia to India, Sri Lanka, and China. Merchants, monks, and scholars carried Buddhist scriptures and philosophies along these networks, introducing new ideas into the region. At first, Mahayana Buddhism did not replace Hinduism but rather was integrated into the existing frameworks of the empire. Hindu deities coexisted with Buddhist bodhisattva figures. Temples like Angkor Wat, originally dedicated to Vishnu, later also bore Buddhist influences.

This shift was more than just a change of deities; it was a metamorphosis of the soul, affecting how people were ruled, lived, and functioned. It was also a move from direct hierarchical rule of the gods and their representatives to the Buddha's emphasis on personal enlightenment, compassion, and the impermanence of life. These teachings resonated deeply with the people, leading to a spiritual renaissance. Monuments began to reflect this change, as Buddhist motifs and symbols began to adorn them.

THE SUKHOTHAI KINGDOM

During this pivotal era, the landscape of Siam was a vibrant patchwork of small city-states and fluctuating kingdoms. Some regions were fully under the control of the expansive Khmer Empire, while others yearned for independence. It was against this backdrop that the Sukhothai Kingdom emerged in 1238 in a moment that can be defined as the golden age of Thai civilization. This name translates to "Dawn of Happiness," appropriately capturing the essence of this new beginning. Situated in what is now north-central Thailand, Sukhothai was initially a thriving trade hub within the Lavo region under Khmer dominion.

The winds of change were set in motion by a local leader named Pho Khun Bang Klang Hao, who mobilized his people to fight back against their Khmer overlords. The Khmer people were well equipped for warfare, so the Sukhothai rebels must have been better trained and more courageous to have strategically beat their oppressors. This is the first recorded instance of the Thai people using combat to liberate their land and achieve self-determination. (In this context, I use *Thai* to refer to the Tai people, the ethnolinguistic group that formed the Thai kingdoms and ultimately led to the establishment of Thailand as a nation.)

Pho Khun Bang Klang Hao was crowned king with the new name and title of "Sri Indraditya." Sri Indraditya combines Sanskrit's grace with Hindu mythology's power—*Sri* for "radiance," *Indra* for the king of gods, and *Aditya* for the sun god. Thus, the founder of what would be the Phra Ruang dynasty was seen as a leader with the wisdom and power of the king of the gods and the vitality of the life-giving sun.

Sri Indraditya's rule transformed Sukhothai from a Khmer outpost to a prosperous kingdom in its own right. He laid down governance principles focusing on the people's welfare and the land's prosperity, propelling Sukhothai into a period of cultural and economic development. With his enlightened leadership, a new era paved the way for the growth and prosperity of Thai civilization.

The high point of the Sukhothai Kingdom was achieved under the reign of King Ram Khamhaeng the Great, ruling from 1279 to 1298. He was the third monarch of Sukhothai and a pivotal figure in Thai history. His reign saw great expansion of the kingdom's territory—extending its influence over much of what is now central and northern Thailand, parts of Laos, Myanmar (Lower Burma), and the Malay Peninsula—as well as the enhancement of its influence in Southeast Asia through diplomatic successes. He elevated Theravada Buddhism as the spiritual and cultural foundation of Thailand, built temples, and promoted Buddhist teachings, unifying and shaping the kingdom's religious identity. Buddhism was already part of ancient Siam (modern-day Thailand), and the people had begun embracing it as their main religion around 250 B.C.E., primarily through the influence of Indian traders and missionaries. The initial spread of Theravada Buddhism was facilitated by Buddhist monks sent by Emperor Ashoka of India, who dispatched missionaries across Southeast Asia to share Buddhist teachings.

When the Sukhothai Kingdom specifically adopted Theravada Buddhism, they established a new cultural and religious identity separate from the Khmer Empire, reinforcing their own political independence. Theravada Buddhism emphasized simplicity, monastic discipline, and personal enlightenment, aligning with the kingdom's vision for a righteous ruler (Dhammarja). Another monumental achievement attributed to King Ram Khamhaeng is the creation of the Thai alphabet, drawing from Khmer, Sanskrit, Pali, and Grantha scripts. This innovation was crucial for the country's development, enabling the recording of laws, Buddhist scriptures, and literature, thereby solidifying Thai cultural and national identity. His innovative governance showcased his dedication to fair rule and the well-being of his subjects. One example of this was the introduction of a bell system that allowed commoners direct access to justice. This period is celebrated for its prosperity, expansion, cultural richness, diplomacy, and effective governance.

WHEN MYTH BECOMES HISTORY: THE FOUNDATION OF AYUTTHAYA

While Sukhothai was setting the early foundations of Thai culture, another Thai power was rising to the south. The origin of the kingdom of Ayutthaya is a significant chapter in Thai history, which is a tapestry woven from both historical records and legends. Among these, the story of Prince U Thong, whose name means the "Golden Cradle," stands out, as told through a few distinct narratives. One such tale suggests he was a descendant of the illustrious King Mangrai, the founder of Chiang Mai, who sought refuge and new beginnings in a verdant and strategic area of ancient Siam due to a smallpox outbreak or political turmoil in his homeland.

Upon his arrival in the south, Prince U Thong saw the fertile land cradled by rivers and envisioned a thriving, defensible realm. In 1351, he was crowned King Ramathibodi I, birthing the Ayutthaya Kingdom and a new dynasty. The Thai name *Ramathibodi* translates to "Overlord Rama" in Sanskrit (Ramadhipati) and continues to serve as a formal title for Thai monarchs. Embedded in this name is the essence of the revered Hindu god Vishnu (Rama) from the ancient Indian epic the Ramayana—an ideal king celebrated for morality, righteousness, and virtue. The inclusion of *bodi* in the title signifies "awakening" or "enlightenment" and commitment to the Buddhist Dharma or teachings; thus, Ramathibodi encapsulates the notion of a ruler serving as a paragon of leadership and moral integrity in the worldviews of both Hinduism and Buddhism. All Thai monarchs have taken Ramathibodi as their formal or ceremonial title, but only a few are widely known by it.

King Ramathibodi I's reign marked a fusion of Khmer and Thai administrative and cultural practices with his new innovative vision for rulership. Legend has it that he named the kingdom Ayutthaya because he was inspired by the sacred Indian city of Ayodhya, which echoes the deep Indian cultural and religious influences, aligning the kingdom with the majestic, righteous, and virtuous themes of the Ramayana, which in Thai became the Ramakien, as well as the earliest form of Buddhism drawing directly from the Pali Canon of India as well. Ramathibodi I's ascendency symbolized more than mere territorial conquest; it signified the establishment of a nuanced societal, administrative, and religious fabric deeply imbued with ethical teachings.

King Ramathibodi I was revered as a semidivine being embodying the dual role of an earthly sovereign and spiritual beacon, guiding his subjects toward a life in harmony with the Dharma. Under his leadership, Ayutthaya quickly flourished into a vital economic and cultural nexus, asserting itself as a formidable force in Southeast Asia. During his reign, he played an important role in spreading the ideology of Theravada Buddhism. With it, he not only shaped governance but also contributed to the development of artistic expression and educational ethos. He worked toward creating a strong and united community founded on the principles of Buddhism. He constructed several temples and played an active role in promoting the faith throughout his kingdom. Under his patronage, Ayutthaya became a hub of art and learning, where literature, sculpture, and architecture reached new heights.

Both the Sukhothai and the Ayutthayan kingdoms were renowned for their impressive temples and palaces, many of which were adorned with elaborate golden spires that glistened in the sun, testament to both their religious devotion and their wealth and power. These structures were intricately designed, combining various architectural influences, including Hindu and Buddhist styles, which reflected the diverse cultural underpinnings of these kingdoms.

The kingdom of Ayutthaya emerged as a formidable enclave encircled by three rivers, the Chao Phraya, the Pasak, and the Lopburi, and surrounded by rice terraces. This geographic advantage not only fortified it against invaders but also fostered trade, bringing immense wealth and diverse influences into the kingdom. Unlike Sukhothai's humble beginnings, Ayutthaya was grand from its inception, with ambitious architecture and a

court life that drew traders from as far as China, Japan, and even
Europe.

As the Siamese kingdoms began to rise to a new level of power,
the Khmer Empire faced many new challenges. Internal dis-
putes, economic shifts, and water management issues weakened
its core. Meanwhile, changing tides in trade meant that the sea
routes had grown more important than the land routes they had
always dominated, denting their economic prowess. Amid this,
a spiritual transformation was also underway as more and more
people were embracing the teachings of Theravada Buddhism,
shifting away from the age-old Hindu and Mahayana Buddhist
traditions that once anchored the monarchy's divine rule. From
this, the mighty Angkor, once the heart of the Khmer Empire,
found its dominance waning.

The early Thai states initially existed under the shadow of the
Khmers, often as tributaries or vassals. However, as they grew in
power and confidence, they began to assert their independence,
sometimes clashing militarily with the Khmers.

From Vassals to Victors: The Rise of the Siamese Kingdoms

To the west of the Khmer Empire, the kingdom of Ayutthaya was
rapidly expanding its forces and growing into a powerful nation.
The leaders of Ayutthaya had a strong desire for growth and thus
turned their attention to the wealthy heartlands of the Khmer.
Around eighty years after its founding, and three kings later, King
Borommarachathirat II, also known as King Samphraya of Ayutthaya (r. 1424–48), launched a bold military campaign aimed at
the center of the Khmer Empire.

The Siamese kings had a tradition of riding war elephants into
battle, not only as a formidable military tactic but also as a profound symbol of regal authority and prestige. Elephants—revered

within Thai culture—are symbols of power, wisdom, royalty, divine authority, and national identity. Adorned in regal attire and carefully selected for their qualities, these elephants elevated the morale of the troops and were integral to military strategy.

Positioned strategically around the king's elephant, the Chatulangkabat warriors formed an impenetrable guard. As guardians of the monarch and symbols of righteous and courageous protection, the Chatulangkabat held a place of high honor within the royal court. Typically, four warriors were assigned to protect each leg of the elephant, with a fifth, a specialist commander, positioned at the front protecting the head. This tactical formation ensured the king's safety from all possible threats. Their proximity to the king was a testament to their critical role, and their duty demanded not only exceptional martial prowess but also unyielding loyalty and fortitude. Their rigorous training regimen included mastering the hand-to-hand combat techniques of Muay Boran, utilizing punches, elbows, knees, and kicks, as well as clinching, wrestling, and throwing. Moreover, these guards were adept with various weapons, such as double swords, shields, and spears, and were versed in advanced tactics of warfare. This made them formidable in both defense and offense.

The fusion of the king riding into war with his elite warriors and the sacred war elephants creates a vivid tableau blending Thailand's religious reverence, cultural heritage, and martial tradition.

In 1431, King Borommarachathirat II of Ayutthaya rode into battle atop his mighty war elephant. From this elevated perch, he commanded his troops at the heart of the conflict, embodying for them both the strength of an ancient warrior and the vision of a leader fighting for the liberation of his people. Side by side with his elite warriors and with the full might of his army behind him, King Borommarachathirat led a decisive charge, and together they captured Angkor, the prized heart of the Khmer Empire. This strategic victory not only demonstrated Ayutthaya's military prowess but also cemented the king's legacy as a warrior-leader and protector of the kingdom. It was a significant milestone in reshaping the geopolitical history of Southeast Asia signifying the decline of the Khmer Empire and the ascension of the Thai people and the kingdom of Ayutthaya as a dominant power in the region.

Ayutthaya underwent a period of consolidation, expansion, and cultural development. While there were other emerging kingdoms and dynasties across the region, none possessed the same level of power and influence as the Siamese kingdoms. Ayutthaya stood out as the strongest, with its strategic riverine location and imposing fortifications. It had powerful political influence in the region and was a flourishing, cosmopolitan trade hub, attracting traders from India, Japan, China, Europe, and the Arab world. Ayutthaya's warriors were not only skilled in combat but also deeply knowledgeable about cultural practices and customs. They devoted themselves to rigorous training to be prepared to defend their nation against any potential invaders.

The bustling markets of Ayutthaya were a sign of its abundance and prosperity. The temples and palaces brimmed with art, culture, luxury, and literature. At its peak, Ayutthaya's population is estimated to have reached approximately one million people, testament to its status as a major cultural and economic hub. The kingdom continued to expand and thrive undisputed, and its golden spires and intricate waterways were a beacon of culture across the world.

The Theravadin Buddhist kingdom was a place where literature, sculpture, and architecture reached new heights. Throughout its history, the Ayutthaya Kingdom engaged in extensive trade and diplomatic relations with numerous foreign powers, including its Asian neighbors such as China, Japan, India, and various Southeast Asian kingdoms, as well as European powers like Portugal, the Netherlands, France, and England, all enriching its cultural and commercial landscape.

The Ayutthaya Kingdom stood for over four hundred years—between 1351 and 1767—and at its peak it was one of the largest and most cosmopolitan cities in the world, rivaling London, Paris, and New York in size, wealth, and international influence. Its thriving trade network connected Asia, the Middle East, and Europe, surpassing London and Paris, which were still developing their urban and commercial power. Nestled in the heart of this flourishing kingdom, however, was a narrative of constant vigilance and strategic warfare. Ayutthaya's prosperity attracted numerous internal and external threats, most notably from the Burmese dynasties, leading to centuries of intermittent conflicts that tested the kingdom's resilience and strategic acumen.

In 1767, the Burmese army sacked and destroyed Ayutthaya, burning the city to the ground and marking the end of an era—more of which will be explored in future chapters.

CHAPTER TWO

A THAI SPIRITUAL UNDERSTANDING

ADVERSITY AS A TEST OF CHARACTER

At the age of eight, I embarked on what I believed would be an exciting adventure at a prestigious boarding school nestled in the lush Wiltshire countryside. My family's hope for me to gain more discipline and a superior education was quickly obliterated by the hostility and isolation I experienced. As one of the few students of color in a predominantly white boarding school, I faced daily oppression, racism, and bullying that challenged my naturally confident and adventurous spirit. Even the teachers were hostile. On day one a teacher caught me excitedly jumping on my bed in the dorm. He grabbed me by the scruff of my neck and threw me into the metal bedposts of my bed. In that moment, I realized I wasn't in a safe haven and needed to stay on guard in this unfamiliar place.

However, the resilience I had developed from my family's unconditional love, coupled with my martial arts training, fueled my determination to withstand and confront adversities. Still, the stark contrast between my home environment and the rigid hierarchy of boarding school was a shock. About six months into my first year, I found myself confronted by a big fifteen-year-old bully. His taunts were full of racial slurs, but I shot back a retort that earned laughs from the surrounding students. Enraged, he lunged at me, prompting a chase. It led us to the school garden, where a sequoia tree stood at least one hundred feet tall. I figured if I could just get up there, he'd surely tire and give up. But he didn't.

As I clambered higher, he pursued me, reaching out to try to yank me down. The ground was a long way away as I neared the top, but I had nowhere left to climb. With my pursuer nearly upon me, time seemed to slow down, and my as-yet untapped instincts began to kick in. A rapid calculation, a glance into his relentless eyes, and I made my choice. Letting go, I stepped off of my secure perch and began free-falling down through the tree, plummeting toward the ground before snagging myself on the branches far below him. The shock in his eyes was mirrored by the gasps of the onlooking children on the ground. They stared with a mix of disbelief and admiration as I swiftly descended. As soon as my feet touched the ground the school bell chimed, supporting my strategic retreat as I dashed to my next class, cherishing my momentary triumph. He beat me up when he caught me again later, but my escape that day always stood out more in my mind than his beatings.

The school's outdated disciplinary methods added another layer of adversity for me, with punishments that seemed more akin to psychological warfare than corrective measures.

Being sent to a boarding school from such a young age brought me many challenges, but none as severe as an incident involving a classmate. One day he peppered me with slurs trying to get a rise out of me. Provoked and resolved not to let it slide, I chased him. In a sudden turn, he slammed a glass door in my direction. Reacting instinctively, I reached out to stop it, but the glass shattered under the impact. This severed the main artery, critical nerves, and tendons in my wrist, resulting in significant blood loss. In the hospital, I underwent four hours of microsurgery as doctors meticulously repaired the extensive damage.

My family withdrew me from the school, finally realizing that it wasn't a safe place for me, and for the rest of the year, I began to recover. As the days turned into weeks, the wound began to heal, but what was left behind was the mental trauma and the thirteen-stitch scar across my wrist. My strong and coordinated hand was now weak and lacked control. With little guidance on physical therapy and rehabilitation, I had to adapt.

Determined to persevere, I hid my injury and began using my left hand for most tasks. I eventually became somewhat ambidextrous, employing both hands for things but not perfectly. Over time, I buried the traumatic memory within, and to many, my challenges remained hidden. But behind closed doors, every simple task from dressing in the morning or after sports to writing notes or catching a ball became a test of my resilience.

THAI SPIRITUAL COSMOLOGY

Thai culture is deeply rooted in a unique blend of Theravada Buddhism, Hinduism, and traditional animistic beliefs from the region. These diverse cosmologies find a profound expression in Thailand's national epic, the Ramakien. This adaptation of the Ramayana, a pivotal Hindu epic, integrates and reshapes the foreign influences of this Indian classic to reflect the country's own distinct beliefs, values, and traditions. The Ramakien is more than a mythical narrative; it's a source of Thailand's moral lessons, spiritual insights, and cultural values, tailored to resonate deeply with Thai society.

The Ramakien's influence is omnipresent, shaping various aspects of royal authority and cultural expression, including traditional dance, music, art—and crucially, the martial arts of Muay Boran and Muay Thai. These martial arts draw upon the epic's themes of bravery, strategy, intelligence, honor, and spiritual strength and mirrors these principles and values in their practices and ethos.

The cosmology presented in the Ramakien is intricate and multidimensional. It portrays a universe composed of three distinct realms:

- The heavenly realm of the gods and celestial beings, ruled by Indra, the king of the gods, known in Thai as Phra In,
- The earthly realm of humans and animals, a transformative abode of physical experience and spiritual journeys.
- The underworld, home to demonic entities, serving as a realm of shadows and retribution, where spirits are confronted with the consequences of their past actions and their struggles unfold in the depths of darkness.

This basic structure is enriched by multiple heavenly realms and hellish realms into which beings can ascend or descend as depicted in both Hindu and Buddhist cosmologies, each with its unique deities and beings. It reflects a worldview presenting a universe that's diverse and multilayered, governed by an array of deities and spiritual beings.

Based on Hindu influences, there is a divine hierarchy of gods that oversee this universe, each with distinct roles and attributes. The exact number of gods and goddesses is vast—and often said to be infinite. Yet central to this pantheon is the Hindu triumvirate of Brahma, Vishnu, and Shiva, symbolizing creation, preservation, and destruction. The religion also encompasses a wide array of male and female deities, ranging from the major gods to a myriad of local and regional deities.

Brahma

In Thailand, Brahma is known as Phra Phrom, and he is celebrated as the creator, holding a more prominent place than in Indian Hinduism. He is depicted with four faces, each of which symbolizes one of the four directions of north, east, south, and west and together denoting his omnipresence; therefore, he can see and protect everything in both the human and heavenly realms. The Erawan Temple in Bangkok is a popular Phra Phrom shrine for new beginnings and blessings.

Vishnu

Vishnu is known as Phra Narai in Thailand, and he is revered in his role as preserver and protector of the universe and for maintaining cosmic order. His incarnations, especially as Rama from the Ramakien, are not only religious figures and royalty but also cultural heroes, influencing Thai literature, dance, and art with a unique local interpretation of these mythological narratives. The largest Phra Narai temple in Thailand is Wat Phra Narai Maharat located in Nakhon Ratchasima. This significant temple features a unique building on an island surrounded by a small lake, which houses a revered sandstone statue of Phra Narai.

Shiva

Shiva is known as Phra Isuan in Thailand, and he represents destruction and regeneration. His role in the cosmic cycle is crucial for universal balance. While less prominent than Phra Phrom or Phra Narai, Phra Isuan's influence in Thai culture is significant, particularly in self-discipline and the arts, with his attributes reflected in traditional Thai dance forms. The Devasathan in Bangkok is the site of the largest shrine dedicated to Phra Isuan and the official center of Hinduism in Thailand. It is home to a group of Hindu priests called the Royal Thai Brahmins who trace their ancestry back to Rameswaram in Tamil Nadu, India, and play a crucial role in maintaining the traditions and rituals of Hinduism in Thailand, especially within royal and ceremonial contexts.

Together Phra Phrom, Phra Narai, and Phra Isuan embody the dynamic and syncretic nature of Thai religious practice, where Hindu deities are seamlessly woven into the fabric of cultural and spiritual life. Their stories, symbols, and roles have been adapted to fit the Thai context, reflecting the unique way that Thais have embraced and reinterpreted Hindu gods within their own cultural and religious expression. For example, Brahma is associated with the realm of Brahmaloka, one of the highest heavenly realms in the spiritual hierarchy, where beings experience profound peace and enlightenment. In Hinduism, this is seen as a place of liberation reserved for souls who have attained a significant level of spiritual advancement. However, in Thai Buddhism, even the sublimest realms, including Brahmaloka, are within the cycle of birth, death, and rebirth. In this view, Brahmaloka is a realm attainable through advanced meditation and good karma, but it is not the ultimate goal.

In this we see the influence of Buddhist philosophy: deities exist but are not viewed as supreme. Instead, Buddhism emphasizes the law of karma, which connects actions and consequences, and the Dharma, which are the Buddha's teachings and the path to enlightenment.

Siddhartha Gautama

Siddhartha Gautama, commonly known as the Buddha, is not worshipped as a god but rather revered as an enlightened teacher. The Buddha is honored as a supreme figure, but his role is not that of a creator or overseer of the universe. His teachings form the foundation of religious practice, moral conduct, and the pursuit of spiritual awareness because he discovered and shared a path to enlightenment, which he taught leads to the end of suffering and the cycle of reincarnation. Ultimately, the Buddhist path is designed to help practitioners ascend to nirvana, a state of perfect peace and happiness free from suffering and desire. In nirvana, individual consciousness comes to an end, and there is no longer a sense of a separate self or ego.

PRINCIPLES OF COSMIC ORDER

In the Southeast Asian worldview, the earthly and spiritual realms are deeply intertwined, with animistic, Hindu, and Buddhist influences merging within a Buddhist framework. This synthesis brings together the Buddha's teachings, known as the Dharma, alongside the concepts of karma, reincarnation, and multiple realms connected by Mount Sumeru, the cosmic mountain that links all realms of existence. This fusion creates a spiritual understanding where various beliefs combine, shaping the way of life, death, rebirth, and all the universe.

Dharma

In Hinduism, the term *dharma* refers to an individual's duty, righteousness, and the moral order of the universe. In Buddhism, it denotes the teachings of the Buddha, which reflect how to live in accordance with the laws of the universe and walk the path to enlightenment. Overall in both, Dharma encompasses duty and morality, representing the righteous path that guides individuals in their actions and decisions.

Karma

Both Hinduism and Buddhism emphasize karma, the law of cause and effect, by which every action has a consequence that will manifest in the future, either in this life or in future lives. Karma, in Hinduism, is closely associated with the continuous round of birth, death, and rebirth—*samsara*—with karma determining the nature of one's existence. It decides whether a person will ascend or descend to the heavenly, earthly, or hellish realms, depending on their actions. Such possibilities underscore the importance of living a righteous life, adhering to one's own dharma (duty, moral law), and pursuing the path of righteousness to achieve liberation from the cycle of existence. In Buddhism, the concept of karma is more focused on the present moment and the immediate causality of actions, thoughts, and intentions. It emphasizes the importance of mindful living, ethical conduct, and the cultivation of positive mental states to break free from suffering and rebirth, ultimately leading to nirvana. Each person's daily actions affect their karma and thus determine their fate in the future of their existence.

Samsara and Reincarnation

In both Hinduism and Buddhism, the cycle of birth, death, and rebirth known as samsara is key, and the goal is to escape it. In Hinduism, this escape, called *moksha,* involves the soul (*atman*) merging with the divine (Brahman) through righteous living and self-realization. Buddhism seeks to end suffering and achieve nirvana by understanding that there is no permanent self (*anatta*) and focusing on ethical behavior, meditation, and wisdom. Both religions emphasize moral conduct and spiritual practice to break free from samsara.

Mount Sumeru (Meru)

In Hindu and Buddhist cosmologies, there is an extraordinary sacred mountain called Mount Meru, known in Thai as Sumeru. Envisioned as the axis mundi—the center around which the entire universe is structured—Mount Sumeru transcends mere geographical conception. It is a colossal mountain, revered as the focal point of both the physical and metaphysical universes. This sacred mountain is not only the highest point in the cosmic landscape but also a central figure in the spiritual journey.

In the physical sense, Mount Sumeru is imagined as immensely high, dwarfing the surrounding landscapes. It is traditionally believed to be the pivot around which celestial bodies like the sun, moon, and stars orbit. This physical centrality places it at the core of the universe, towering above the various heavenly realms. The mountain's base is thought to be anchored in the earthly realm, while its summit extends into the loftiest heavens, symbolizing a connection between the terrestrial and the celestial. In Hinduism, Mount Sumeru is believed to be the abode of Indra, the king of gods. In Buddhism, Indra is known as Śakra and considered a defender of the Dharma and a leader of celestial beings. He is highly respected for his dedication to the Buddha and his teachings. In Buddhist tales, he is often depicted as a protective deity who supports the virtuous and the faithful.

Symbolically, Mount Sumeru's significance is multifaceted. The mountain serves as a bridge, linking the distinct realms of existence and connecting the human world with the divine domains of gods and celestial beings. But the metaphorical aspect of Mount Sumeru is perhaps its most profound. Climbing Mount Sumeru is often viewed as a symbolic journey that signifies the ascent from the mundane to the divine, from earthly confines to spiritual liberation. In this way, Mount Sumeru becomes more than a mythological construct, representing the path to spiritual awakening and the pursuit of enlightenment.

THAI BUDDHIST REALMS OF EXISTENCE

The Thai Buddhist cosmology presents a fascinating tapestry of existence, encompassing a spectrum of realms from celestial highs to infernal lows. Each realm—be it heavenly, earthly, or hellish—mirrors a distinct set of experiences and conditions profoundly influenced by the actions and consequences of a person's karma. One can also view these various realms as diverse states of consciousness or awareness.

Heavenly Realms (Sawan)

Brahma Realms (Brahmaloka): These highest realms epitomize spiritual ecstasy and profound meditative accomplishments. Inhabited by beings called brahmas, these realms offer refined states of bliss yet are still impermanent in nature. They're not the ultimate destination but rather stepping stones in the journey toward nirvana or the transcendence of all realms.

Deva Realms (Davadusintawat): Home to celestial beings and gods known as devas, these realms are characterized by extraordinary beauty, pleasure, and longevity. Despite their allure, they too are transient and part of the cyclical existence of birth, death, and rebirth.

Asura Realm (Asurawat): Home to the demigods known as asuras, this is a world full of supernatural wonder, passion, envy, and perpetual conflict. While these beings exhibit divine powers, they are also plagued by negative emotions and constant battles, especially with the devas. Despite their divine traits, asuras are often embroiled in conflicts and struggles with other beings.

Earthly Realms

Manusya Realm (Manussaloka): The human realm is marked by a blend of joy and sorrow: the human experience offers a unique balance conducive to spiritual growth and enlightenment. The ability for moral decision-making and karmic accumulation defines human existence.

Tiryagyoni Realm (Tiracchānayoni): The animal realm is characterized by ignorance and instinctual behavior. This realm is where beings experience the harsh existence of animals dominated by survival challenges and a lack of complex intellectual or spiritual pursuits.

Hellish Realms

Preta Realm (Petaloka): The hungry ghosts realm is inhabited by pretas or hungry ghosts: this realm symbolizes intense unfulfilled cravings and desires. These beings suffer from insatiable hunger and thirst, a metaphor for greed and obsession.

Naraka Realm (Naraka): The lowest of hellish realms is the domain of intense suffering, a temporary but severe consequence for grave unwholesome actions. The pain here is a direct reflection of the negative karma accumulated from serious misdeeds.

Nirvana

Beyond all these realms exists nirvana, the pinnacle of spiritual achievement and the cessation of all suffering. It's not an escape, but an awakening to the ultimate truth, free from the illusions of self and the endless cycle of birth and death. Achieving nirvana is synonymous with enlightenment, a state of complete understanding and liberation.

In this intricate and profound belief system, each realm reflects the consequence¡s of one's actions and choices, underscoring the Buddhist aim to transcend the cycle of rebirth and attain the ultimate peace of nirvana. Each of these realms may be regarded either as a tangible location or as a particular mental state or life path based on karma. This complex and layered picture of reality as depicted in the Ramakien resonates deeply within Thai society and is reflected in the everyday life and practices of the Thai people. It not only deeply influences the human journey but also profoundly shapes Thailand's cultural and spiritual fabric. This perspective merging animist spirituality and Hindu mythology with Buddhism reveals a complex worldview where the spiritual and the material realms, alongside divine and demonic forces, harmoniously coexist, each governed by distinct principles and entities, yet intricately interconnected through the universal doctrines of karma and Dharma.

UNDERSTANDING BUDDHISM

Siddhartha Gautama: The Awakening of the Buddha

Siddhartha Gautama was a prince born in India into the Kshatriya caste, which was traditionally associated with warriors and rulers. As a prince, he lived a sheltered life inside a beautiful palace with the best of everything, but as an adult, he encountered the suffering that existed in the world beyond the palace walls. Seeking an end to this suffering, he renounced his royal luxuries to live a spiritual life with minimal possessions or pleasures. After years of practice, meditation, fasting, and devout service, he found no true answers. Yet as his journey continued, he eventually achieved enlightenment after meditating deeply under a bodhi tree for a long time. He then became known as the Buddha, meaning the "Awakened One." The term *buddha* is a sacred title given to those who have attained the highest level of spiritual awakening in Buddhism. He then began to teach this middle path he had followed for others to find enlightenment and freedom from suffering.

The Buddha's teachings were clear and accessible, often drawing upon vivid imagery to convey deeper truths. In some ways, one could say that the Buddha, raised in a caste of warriors and rulers, brought a warrior's sensibility to his teachings. He frequently used examples of warriors, archers, and trained animals to illustrate his insights on self-discipline and inner mastery. These metaphors emphasized the importance of taming and controlling the mind, much like a warrior controls weapons or an animal is trained for battle.

For example, in the Dhammapada, he states:

> Just as an archer might make straight the arrow, so the wise man makes straight the trembling, unsteady mind, which is difficult to guard and difficult to restrain.
> —DHAMMAPADA, VERSE 33

He also draws comparisons between tamed animals and the disciplined individual:

> The tamed elephant is led to battle. The king mounts a tamed horse. The tamed person is the one who endures abuse. He is fit to serve the community.
> —DHAMMAPADA, VERSE 322

Further reinforcing this theme of inner conquest, the Buddha famously taught:

> Though one should conquer a thousand times a thousand men in battle, yet he indeed is the noblest victor who conquers himself.
> —DHAMMAPADA, VERSE 103

These verses highlight the Buddha's view that true victory is not found in defeating external enemies, but in mastering one's own mind, emotions, and desires—a process requiring the same level of skill, patience, and discipline as training for battle.

Just as Muay Boran warriors disciplined their bodies and minds to achieve peak physical and mental resilience, the Buddha taught that mastery over one's thoughts and actions was key to breaking free from the cycle of suffering and reaching nirvana, and he provided clear and practical instructions on how to overcome suffering and attain enlightenment. The Buddha's teachings are not dogmatic; they are offered instead as tools for individuals to investigate and experience for themselves. The ultimate goal is to achieve insight into the nature of reality, leading to liberation.

The Buddha's foundational teachings are centered on the Four Noble Truths and the Noble Eightfold Path, which offer a comprehensive guide to understanding and overcoming suffering and leading to enlightenment. These teachings serve as the cornerstone of Buddhist practice and philosophy, providing clear insight into the nature of existence and the path to spiritual liberation.

> The best of paths is the Eightfold Path. The best of truths are the Four Noble Truths. The best of states is freedom from attachment. The best of men is the one who sees.
>
> —DHAMMAPADA, VERSE 273

The Four Noble Truths

The Four Noble Truths outline the reality of human suffering and the way to transcend it:

1. **The Truth of Suffering** (*Dukkha*): Life is permeated by suffering, whether through birth, aging, sickness,

or death. Even moments of happiness are fleeting and ultimately give way to dissatisfaction.

2. **The Truth of the Cause of Suffering** (*Samudaya*): Suffering is caused by desire and attachment. Craving, whether for pleasure, material goods, or immortality, binds us to a cycle of suffering.

3. **The Truth of the Cessation of Suffering** (*Nirodha*): The cessation of suffering is possible by letting go of craving and attachment. When these are extinguished, suffering naturally comes to an end, leading to a state of peace—nirvana.

4. **The Truth of the Path to the Cessation of Suffering** (*Magga*): The way to the cessation of suffering is through the Noble Eightfold Path, which outlines a practical approach to ethical conduct, mental discipline, and wisdom.

Together, the Four Noble Truths and the Noble Eightfold Path form a complete guide to overcoming suffering and achieving enlightenment. As the Buddha emphasized:

He who walks in the Noble Eightfold Path with unswerving determination is sure to reach the end of suffering.

—DHAMMAPADA, VERSE 275

The Noble Eightfold Path

The Noble Eightfold Path is the road map to the cessation of suffering, offering guidance on how to live a life that cultivates wisdom, ethical conduct, and mental discipline:

1. **Right View** (*Samma Ditthi*): Understanding the Four Noble Truths and seeing reality as it truly is.

2. **Right Intention** (*Samma Sankappa*): Cultivating thoughts of renunciation, goodwill, and harmlessness.

3. **Right Speech** *(Samma Vaca)*: Speaking truthfully, kindly, and avoiding harmful speech.

4. **Right Action** (*Samma Kammanta*): Acting ethically and avoiding harm to others.

5. **Right Livelihood** (*Samma Ajiva*): Earning a living in a way that does not cause harm or suffering to others.

6. **Right Effort** (*Samma Vayama*): Making an effort to abandon unwholesome states and cultivate wholesome ones.

7. **Right Mindfulness** (*Samma Sati*): Being fully aware of one's body, feelings, mind, and mental states.

8. **Right Concentration** (*Samma Samadhi*): Developing deep concentration through meditation to cultivate mental focus and tranquility.

The wise man makes straight the trembling, unsteady mind, which is difficult to guard and difficult to restrain.

—DHAMMAPADA, VERSE 33

Just as attempting a task without the right tools can make it difficult, navigating life without proper awareness and understanding can feel overwhelming. The Buddha's teachings offer practical tools and techniques for walking the path of enlightenment, but these insights aren't handed to us; they must be discovered through personal exploration, experience, and reflection. It is through trial, error, and mindful practice that one can truly unlock the wisdom needed to overcome life's challenges and find inner peace.

CHAPTER THREE

MYTHS AND LEGENDS OF THAI MARTIAL TRADITIONS

TRIALS AND TRIBULATIONS

My nomadic educational journey included everything from an inner-city primary school to a countryside primary to various boarding schools to a public school, a referral unit, and finally, a college. While the schools varied, the racial and social challenges remained constant. On top of that, adjusting to life with a severe hand injury further complicated both my studies and athletic pursuits.

Despite all this, I managed to thrive in sports like basketball, rugby, and cricket, channeling my energy into these physical endeavors. I always found comfort in spending time in nature and enjoyed exploring various subjects, from geography and art to history, mathematics, drama, and religious studies.

When I was eleven, I was back living with my mum in a place not far from Taunton, Somerset, and I had the opportunity to rekindle my passion for martial arts. The only thing on offer was judo, and although my weakened right grip made it a struggle to grip an opponent's gi, I persevered. Though my time with judo was short, I mastered some effective throws and developed more mental fortitude to recover from setbacks. Overall, it deepened my passion for pursuing a martial discipline that truly resonated with me.

A year later we moved to the mystical town of Glastonbury, Somerset. I found myself drawn to the world of boxing, captivated by the amazing feats of champions such as Muhammad Ali, Mike Tyson, and Lennox Lewis. The allure of a fresh challenge and gaining new skills drew me into the ring. Although my hand still didn't work properly, I had learned to adapt and form a rudimentary fist. Boxing's rhythmic dance of jabs, footwork, power, and strategy fascinated me. The training was tough, but I genuinely loved it. However, my trainer's attitude made it an unpleasant experience. He was a mean guy and took pleasure in letting his far more experienced sons rough me up during every class while offering me little instruction or guidance.

When I was sixteen, my mother and I returned to London. I was thrilled to be back in the big city, but it soon became evident that London and the countryside were worlds apart culturally. I had been surrounded by predominantly English people in the countryside, but London exposed me to much more diversity.

In this new environment, every aspect of my identity, from my clothing style to my taste in music and even my way of speaking, could be scrutinized as a marker of social status. After my dad relocated to Miami, Florida, during my teenage years, I found myself even more influenced by American TV shows, films, and music, which shaped my cultural preferences. While I had always been into hip-hop and liked baggy clothing, the people I met at college were more inclined toward genres like drum and bass, jungle music, UK rap, and garage, and they didn't typically sport American-style clothing. Adaptation was my weapon, a crucial skill, and I had to learn to adjust if I wanted to find my way as quickly as possible.

London was tense, and male aggression seemed to be at an all-time high. People would sometimes pick fights for the slightest reasons, like making prolonged eye contact. I had to learn the delicate balance between exuding confidence and strength without inadvertently provoking confrontations. Gang culture, drug issues, and crime were also more overtly present here than in the places I had lived previously.

THE RAMAKIEN—BATTLE OF GOOD VS. EVIL

The Ramakien is a harmonious blending of history with myth reimagined to embody the essence of Thai beliefs and traditions. It's a tale that has influenced not just the art and literature of Thailand, but the revered martial arts of Muay Boran and Muay Thai.

Originally known as the Ramayana in India, the epic's journey to Thailand traces back to as early as the thirteenth century, and from there it embedded itself into the cultural and spiritual heart and soul of the region. However, the destruction of Ayutthaya in 1767 resulted in the loss of many ancient manuscripts, including earlier versions of this tale. It wasn't until the late eighteenth century, between 1785 and 1807 and under the watchful eye of King Rama I of the Chakri dynasty, that the Ramakien as it is known today was meticulously compiled. This newer version serves as a testament to Thailand's resilience and dedication to preserving its rich cultural heritage amid adversity. The rendition of the Ramakien presented in this book is a condensed adaptation, crafted from the comprehensive version established during Rama I's reign.

To fully grasp the setting of this tale, it's crucial to recognize that the universe is divided into three main realms: the heavenly, the earthly, and the underworld—as outlined in the previous chapter. These realms form the foundational structure of the narrative's universe, each hosting unique entities and governed by distinct laws that frame the backdrop against which the story unfolds. The universe in totality is a place rich in contrasts and duality, where cosmic forces of good and evil, order and chaos, creation and destruction continuously interact. This universe also operates under the natural cycle of birth, existence, death, transformation, and rebirth all governed by the cosmic laws of karma, Dharma, and the celestial beings.

I present this condensed retelling to encapsulate the epic's essence and vitality and as a window into the profound significance the Ramakien holds within Thai heritage, especially its influence on the nation's martial arts traditions.

THE RAMAKIEN RETOLD:
HEROES, HUMANS, AND DEMONS

Phra Phrom (Lord Brahma), the creator god, rules over all of the realms with love and compassion, offering blessings to all who walk the path of righteousness, whether they be humans, divine beings, asuras, demons, or lost souls—even those known for their malevolent ways. He is a fair and just ruler who seeks to support all of creation. Central to this cosmic dance are Phra Isuan (Shiva), the deity of destruction, and Phra Narai (Vishnu), the preserver. Together they maintain the universe's balance, ensuring that neither chaos nor order predominates. Phra Narai, particularly, plays a crucial role in restoring equilibrium during times of disruption. He descends to the earthly realm in various avatars, intervening whenever the asuras—beings driven by base desires like lust, greed, and envy—threaten to overpower the forces of good.

At the center of this cosmic drama is the majestic Mount Sumeru, the deeply revered mythical mountain that anchors all realms—physical, metaphysical, and spiritual. It is envisaged as the pivotal axis around which all cosmic planes orbit. It serves not only as a physical and metaphysical landmark but also as a symbol of universal order and harmony, around which the dance of divine and mortal realms unfolds.

During an era of great tranquility across the realms, the winds of change began to whisper, heralding an era of upheaval. It was during this time that a child was born, Tosakan (Ravana), to a wise man named Vishrava and a demon princess named Kaikesi. This lineage made Tosakan a blend of contrasts: part demon from his mother's heritage and part sage through his father's lineage. This unique combination bestowed upon Tosakan extraordinary gifts that set him apart from both regular humans and celestial beings.

Tosakan was not just a product of his heritage but also of his unparalleled devotion to Phra Isuan. His dedication was such that it moved the heavens, compelling Phra Isuan and other deities to bestow upon him boons of immense power. These boons were not mere tokens, but transformative gifts that endowed Tosakan with formidable abilities, making him a daunting force revered and feared in equal measure.

These divine gifts, in the fabric of celestial narratives, are akin to milestones that shape the destinies of those who receive them. They represent pivotal moments where divine favor intersects with mortal endeavor, often changing the course of history itself.

Tosakan's rise to power was marked by an insatiable ambition and an overwhelming sense of invincibility fueled by his unmatched intellect and supernatural gifts. His relentless pursuit of dominance knew no bounds, driving him to extend his reign across the earthly, underworld, and even heavenly realms. With each conquest, his empire expanded, but so too did the shadow he cast across the cosmos. His son, Ranapak, followed in his father's footsteps, amplifying the trail of destruction by challenging the celestial order itself. Ranapak's audacity to confront Phra In (Indra), the sovereign of the heavenly realms, sent ripples of despair among the gods and celestial beings. The balance of power shifted dramatically as Tosakan asserted his dominion over the three realms, establishing an era of dread and awe.

At the heart of Tosakan's empire lay Lanka, a city of unparalleled splendor and wealth, often linked to the historical island of Sri Lanka. Legend holds that Lanka was originally crafted by the divine architect Vishwakarma for the gods. It was later taken over by Kubera, the god of wealth and Tosakan's half brother. However, through cunning and the use of his supernatural prowess, Tosakan seized Lanka for himself, transforming it into the seat of his vast empire. From Lanka, Tosakan ruled with an iron fist, his authority unchallenged by god, human, or demon. His reign was a testament to the intoxicating lure of power and the peril it poses when unchecked, serving as a cautionary tale of ambition's potential to corrupt even the most gifted of beings.

During Tosakan's reign, his boundless ambition and desire for supremacy drove him to the peak of power, making him the Demon King—a ruler with complete authority over all domains. His metamorphosis was characterized not only by his insatiable greed and towering ego but also by his uniquely demonic appearance. His skin, glowing with an eerie dark bluish-green hue, set him apart from mortals. This unique coloration, a vivid representation of his lineage, added to his regal aura and the mystique of his formidable presence. Tosakan was adorned with ten heads that represented his exceptional intellect, wisdom, and boundless ambition. Each of his heads contained knowledge and cunning, showcasing his strategic abilities and deep understanding of the cosmos. With multiple arms, each wielding a different weapon, he demonstrated his unparalleled martial skills and readiness for battle, emphasizing his dominance in the art of war. His mix of demonic features and royal elegance made him both awe-inspiring and terrifying, encapsulating his ability to both enchant and corrupt. His attire, richly embellished with jewels and fine fabrics, reflected his unrivaled status as the ruler of all the realms.

THE BIRTH OF A GOD:
PHRA NARAI INCARNATED INTO PHRA RAM

As chaos enveloped the realms, a collective plea for salvation arose from the great sages and celestial beings, reaching the ears of Phra Isuan, the deity of destruction and rejuvenation. Recognizing the dire need for divine intervention to restore balance, Phra Isuan summoned Phra Narai, the preserver and protector, to undertake a momentous mission in the earthly realm. To counteract the tumult wrought by Tosakan's reign, Phra Narai chose to reincarnate on this plane as Prince Phra Ram, son of King Dasaratha in the illustrious Ayutthaya Kingdom. This incarnation was no ordinary event: Phra Ram was the fusion of celestial essence and human valor, a harmonious blend of divine grace and earthly virtues.

Phra Ram's journey from princely youth to legendary hero was marked by his exceptional prowess in statecraft and martial arts, making him an unparalleled warrior in his time. His deeds of valor, especially his fearless confrontations with demons, the asuras, and the unjust, carved his name in history as a symbol of resistance against the malevolent forces of Tosakan. Phra Ram's presence became a beacon of hope, illuminating for all the path to liberation from tyranny and oppression, embodying the divine mission entrusted to him by Phra Isuan.

In his youth, Phra Ram was summoned to a majestic ceremony hosted by King Janaka. This grand event was a gathering of suitors from across various kingdoms, each vying for the hand of the king's daughter Princess Sida (Sita). The challenge was to lift and string the formidable Bow of Lord Shiva, a task deemed possible only for the truly worthy.

As suitor after suitor struggled and failed to even budge the bow, anticipation grew. When Phra Ram, along with his brother Pha Lak and their companions, made their entrance, they were immediately struck by Sida's ethereal beauty and poise. The moment Phra Ram approached the bow, a hush fell over the assembly. With a grace that belied the task's difficulty, Phra Ram not only lifted but also effortlessly strung the bow, sealing his fate with Sida in a moment divinely orchestrated.

The Wife of a God

Princess Sida, celebrated for her unparalleled beauty, was equally revered for her wisdom, intellect, and unwavering loyalty. Her virtues made her an ideal consort for the princely hero Phra Ram. Their union, marked by mutual respect and deep affection, was destined to be the foundation of a partnership that would face the trials of time.

This new chapter in their lives was marred by an unexpected decree from King Dasaratha for Phra Ram to take vows and go into a life of monkhood. This order stemmed from the cunning maneuvers of one of the king's wives named Queen Kaikeyi. Her ambitions for her own son to take the throne cast a shadow over Phra Ram's immediate future. Yet bound by a sacred vow his father had unwittingly made to Kaikeyi, Phra Ram embraced his destiny with a stoic resolve that mirrored his deep adherence to the principles of Dharma.

In this moment of upheaval, Phra Ram's journey into monk-hood was not undertaken alone. His brother Pha Lak and his wife Sida, in acts of profound loyalty and love, chose to share in his exile. Together they ventured into the unknown, their path fraught with perils and adversaries that tested their resolve at every turn.

Their odyssey through the dense and perilous wilderness was more than a physical journey; it was a profound quest toward spiritual enlightenment. Venturing into the forest was not merely an exile but a symbolic renunciation of worldly attachments, akin to the path of a monk and sage retreating into nature to gain deeper wisdom free from distractions. The wilderness itself represents a testing ground, filled with demons, hardships, and temptations that would challenge their resolve and strengthen their discipline, virtue, and understanding of the Dharma (righteousness). Amid the lurking dangers and ethereal entities, they maintained their righteousness, embodying the virtues of patience, fortitude, and unwavering faith. This period of trials and tribulations not only deepened their bonds but also refined their characters, fashioning them into beings of moral excellence and high principles.

Guided by destiny, their journey brought them to the serene banks of the Kotawaree River, where a divine encounter awaited. Here, they were graced by the presence of Phra Isuan, who—moved by their unwavering commitment to righteousness—bestowed his blessings upon them. Empowered by this celestial favor, Phra Ram, Pha Lak, and Sida set out to create a sanctuary in the heart of the wilderness. Within this holy enclosure, they dedicated themselves to the rigorous disciplines of spiritual life: fasting, meditation, and the relentless pursuit of wisdom. They delved deep into the essence of the Dharma, strengthening their resolve and fortifying their inner selves against the trials that lay ahead.

Temptations of a Demoness

While he immersed himself in the simple mundane tasks of daily life, Phra Ram's presence in the forest did not go unnoticed. Soorphanaka, the demoness and sister of the formidable Tosakan, laid her eyes on the hermit prince. She was captivated by his effortless strength and serene demeanor amid the wildness. She didn't know who he was, but watching him work hard ignited a fierce desire in her heart. She was captivated by his calmness and expertise and decided to make him hers. Soorphanaka transformed her demonic appearance into the shape of a breathtakingly beautiful woman. With grace and allure, she approached Phra Ram, her intentions veiled behind a facade of gentleness. She offered solace for his weary body, a tender respite from his arduous spiritual endeavors. Her words painted a picture of opulence and power, tempting him with the promise of a prestigious alliance with the mighty kingdom of Lanka.

Yet Phra Ram, steadfast in his dharma and undeterred by earthly desires, gently declined her advances. Angered but undeterred, Soorphanaka retreated into the shadows, her mind obsessed with plots and schemes to capture him. She followed Phra Ram through the forest to his tranquil sanctuary where she saw Sida's radiant beauty and grace. Then a torrent of jealousy and rage surged within Soorphanaka. It became clear to her that as long as Sida was by Phra Ram's side, he would remain beyond her grasp. Consumed by spite, Soorphanaka abandoned all pretense, transforming back into her large fearsome demonic appearance. Intent on eliminating the obstacle to her desires, she launched a vicious assault on their sanctuary with her sights set on destroying Sida. But before her malevolent intentions could inflict any damage, Phra Ram intervened with the agility and precision of a seasoned warrior. He expertly maneuvered to shield Sida, parrying Soorphanaka's ferocious attacks with ease. His counterstrikes, swift and decisive, inflicted grievous wounds on her leg and hand. Pha Lak stepped forward to protect his home from the demoness, but Soorphanaka, in a fit of anger, attacked him fiercely with supernatural punches and kicks, knocking him to the ground. Seeing this, Phra Ram once again quickly intervened, blocking her deadly blows and launching a counterattack with a powerful sword strike that cut her nose from her face. Soorphanaka cried out in pain and ran away defeated, the sound of her screams echoing through the forest.

Upon her return to Lanka, Soorphanaka went to her brother, the Demon King Tosakan, demanding revenge for her mistreatment. As she recounted to him her ordeal, she painted herself as an innocent victim of an unprovoked assault by a man named Phra Ram and his brother Pha Lak. With vivid descriptions, she then spoke of Sida, the most beautiful woman of all the realms, suggesting that she should be one of his brides. Soorphanaka explained that she had wanted to present Sida to him as a gift, only to be brutally attacked before she could succeed. Tosakan's fury at the news of his sister's humiliation was matched only by his intrigue at the mention of Sida's beauty. The idea of claiming the most exquisite woman across all realms as his own ignited a dark desire within him. Tosakan was both angry and drawn by the idea of a potential victory. He became determined to develop a cunning plan to take revenge and acquire a new bride.

In the shadowed halls of Lanka, Tosakan convened with his uncle Khumbhakarna and set a decree to abduct Sida. The mere mention of Phra Ram's name turned Khumbhakarna pale. He had previously clashed with the warrior and narrowly escaped with his life. He stated that Phra Ram wasn't an ordinary mortal. Instead, he was the embodiment of Phra Narai himself, a warrior-god with divine power. Khumbhakarna warned Tosakan by telling him about his own terrifying experience and the fate of his brother who had been slain by Phra Ram.

The Wrath of Tosakan

Tosakan's wrath flared at his uncle's hesitance, which he viewed as a sign of cowardice. With a tyrant's ultimatum, he threatened the annihilation of Khumbhakarna's lineage should he fail in his mission. This command placed Khumbhakarna in a perilous bind, torn between the dread of facing Phra Ram once again and the dire consequences of defying Tosakan's will. Thus burdened by fear yet propelled by the grim stakes set by his nephew, Khumbhakarna set out on a daunting quest to capture Sida.

In their peaceful forest refuge, Phra Ram asked Sida for forgiveness for the danger she had faced while accompanying him. As she replied, her unwavering spirit and their unbreakable bond became apparent. She emphasized that the path of righteousness would always be full of challenges, but they were meant to walk it in unity. Their heartfelt exchange was interrupted by the sight of a mesmerizing golden deer, a vision so captivating that Sida implored Phra Ram to capture it for her. Motivated to fulfill his beloved's wish, he set off on the quest with his brother Pha Lak.

The chase led them deep into the forest, but Phra Ram's keen senses told him that something wasn't right. The golden deer was no more than a malevolent illusion, the demon Khumbhakarna in disguise, attempting to lure them away from their sanctuary. With a perfectly timed and aimed arrow, he pierced the demon's heart, revealing his true identity and killing him instantly. The two brothers hurried back to Sida, but they were too late. Upon their return, the brothers found signs of a fight and realized that Sida was missing. Unbeknownst to the brothers, Tosakan the Demon King had seized her while they were away.

Phra Ram and Pha Lak desperately searched the forest for Sida. The two men looked for hours, calling out her name repeatedly, hoping for a response, but there was only silence and no sign of the princess. As they searched, a troop of monkeys watched from the treetops intrigued by their commotion. Among the troop of monkeys was a powerful and mystical warrior known as Hanuman. He observed the men intently to determine their intent and nature. He was the type to help, but first he had to know if their quest was worthy.

The Legend of Hanuman: A Hero of Heroes

Phra Ram and Pha Lak finally sat down in sorrow beneath the tree, their hearts heavy as the monkeys watched from a distance. Phra Ram, overcome with grief, lamented the loss of his beloved wife Sida. Hanuman watched the men intently, using his keen observational skills, discernment, and wisdom to assess their character. A uniquely powerful being, Hanuman possessed the physical traits of both a monkey and a man, including his iconic tail. Born from divine wind and celestial grace, he was celebrated for his unwavering devotion, righteousness, immense courage, and exceptional skills. Hanuman's commitment to the Dharma guided all his actions as a being of high moral values and integrity. His supernatural powers granted him the ability to alter his size at will and leap across vast distances, so high and far that it seemed as if he could fly. These traits, along with his profound loyalty and unmatched strength, made Hanuman a revered figure, embodying both physical prowess and spiritual devotion. His very presence symbolized a balance of might and morality, inspiring awe and respect in all who encountered him.

As he watched Phra Ram and Pha Lak closely, he recognized their noble qualities and learned about their quest to rescue Sida. He also sensed the divine godly essence of Phra Ram and, realizing that he was the avatar of Phra Narai, offered his assistance, pledging his support as a devoted ally. He knelt before Phra Ram, his eyes ablaze with unwavering loyalty and dedicated himself to helping them save Sida and overthrowing the Demon King Tosakan.

Meanwhile, far across the seas on the distant island of Lanka, Tosakan had taken Sida to his grand city-state where he held her captive in the Ashoka Gardens. He tried to win her over with expensive jewelry and persuasive words, yet Sida remained true to the Dharma and her connection to Phra Ram. When he attempted to assault her, a divine shield enveloped her body, a heavenly gift for her pious prayer and the strength of her will. It burned Tosakan like fire upon contact, pushing him away. He resorted to locking her up in his royal compound guarded by his loyal demoness warriors. Tosakan commanded his army of demons, asuras, mystical creatures, and malevolent humans to stop anyone trying to save the princess.

Upon learning from Hanuman that Sida had been taken across the ocean, Phra Ram felt the challenge to reach her was insurmountable. Hanuman reassured Phra Ram that all would be well and he would find Sida. With a heart brimming with courage, Hanuman vowed to cross the perilous ocean to Lanka and face any threat from Tosakan. His quest was singular: to discover the whereabouts of the noble Sida and whisk her away from the crafty Tosakan.

At the ocean's edge, Hanuman gazed at the daunting expanse before him. With a mighty jump empowered by his father the wind god Vayu, he soared forward and upward like a celestial comet against the blue sky of Southeast Asia. This journey would be full of challenges, as Tosakan's minions were many, and the ocean was home to many dangerous and mythical creatures.

The Serpent of the Sea

As Hanuman soared over the ocean, the calm waters suddenly erupted, revealing a massive sea serpent: Surasa, a divine nagini (serpent woman) with scales shining like polished jade. As their gazes met, he glimpsed a chilling deathliness in her eyes, reminiscent of a primordial predator poised for the kill. Her mouth full of sharp and large teeth darted toward him, attempting to devour him with one bite. The serpent's gigantic and powerful body coiled around Hanuman, trying to capture and crush the nimble monkey warrior. But Hanuman was too swift and strategic. With quick thinking and a great display of agility and cunning, Hanuman dodged the serpent's snapping bites, evading every strike from her venomous teeth with skillful movement and divine speed.

The battle was not just physical—but a test of wits as well. Recognizing the serpent's growing fatigue, Hanuman cleverly led her into a reckless chase. As the serpent lunged furiously trying to stop him, Hanuman deftly maneuvered around her causing her to entangle herself in a sea of knots. With the serpent subdued, Hanuman offered a respectful nod to the creature, acknowledging her strength and role as a guardian of the seas. He then continued on his journey, leaving her to recover and retreat into the ocean's depths. This encounter, brief yet intense, showcased Hanuman's respect for life and his remarkable blend of strength and wisdom.

The Siren's Song

As Hanuman continued his valiant journey across the vast ocean, he encountered a realm where the waters shimmered with an otherworldly glow. From this luminous expanse emerged a sea nymph, ethereal and captivating. Her beauty was such that it seemed to weave the very sea and sky into her allure. Her song, spun from the essence of enchantment itself, was designed to inspire and captivate any heart who heard it. She rose up to ensnare him with it, but Hanuman, steadfast in his mission, remained immune to the siren's spell. He understood the peril hidden in her melodious lure, but instead of confronting it with force, he harmonized with it, showing respect yet not succumbing to the power of the nymph.

As the song climaxed, the siren tried to use all of her powers to enmesh him, but Hanuman's inner strength shone through. The magic broke, not with violence, but with the grace of understanding. The nymph, recognizing Hanuman's unshakable resolve, ceased her song, her eyes reflecting a mix of admiration and respect. With a nod to the sea nymph, Hanuman continued his quest, leaving behind the enchanting echoes of her song. This brief yet poignant encounter highlighted Hanuman's wisdom and his unwavering commitment to his quest, adding another layer of depth to his character.

The Kingdom of Lanka

Upon arriving in Lanka, Hanuman, with the cunning of a seasoned warrior, transformed into a small and subtle form, weaving through Lanka's streets unseen. As he made his way through the palace gardens, his keen senses led him to a secluded grove. It was there that he found Sida, her once radiant spirit now dimmed by the weight of her desperation and hopelessness. Though her purity remained untainted, her captivity had taken a toll on her.

Hanuman revealed himself to the princess. His eyes locked onto hers as he conveyed Phra Ram's promise of liberation and justice. To demonstrate his true allegiance to Phra Ram, he knelt before her and presented her with Phra Ram's ring as a token of recognition and assured her of Phra Ram's unceasing efforts. Although Hanuman offered to rescue her, Sida refused to leave. She reminded him that her honor could only be kept righteous if her husband Phra Ram rescued her himself and defeated the devilish Tosakan. This was the royal protocol that would uphold her dignity. Hanuman rescuing Sida single-handedly could have been perceived as compromising her honor in the societal values of their time.

Sida, in turn, gave Hanuman her hairpin to take back to Phra Ram as proof of her well-being and whereabouts. Hanuman bade the princess farewell and reassured her that he would soon return with Phra Ram and a whole army. Slowly but surely, the light began to return to Sida's eyes, her spirit lifting as Hanuman's words filled her with hope once more.

THE TRIUMPH OF GOOD OVER EVIL

Upon receiving the princess's hairpin, Phra Ram was filled with a mix of emotions—relief at knowing Sida is alive, gratitude toward Hanuman for his successful mission, and a renewed resolve to rescue Sida and defeat Tosakan. Hanuman's detailed account of Sida's condition and the defenses of Lanka also provided Phra Ram and his allies with crucial intelligence for planning their next steps.

This moment also reinforced the bond between Phra Ram and Hanuman, as the monkey warrior had proved his unwavering loyalty and dedication. In preparation for their mission to invade Lanka and defeat Tosakan, Hanuman and Phra Ram work together to gather a mighty army of vanaras (monkey warriors) led by Hanuman and other divine beings loyal to the cause of righteousness. The group held a strategic assembly, carefully planning their approach and tactics for the upcoming battle. With their combined strength and intelligence, they hoped to emerge victorious and bring peace to the land.

The vanaras, endowed with various powers and skills, were pivotal in building a bridge to Lanka and launching the assault against Tosakan's forces. As their army crossed the bridge to

Lanka, Hanuman strategically and swiftly attacked the enemy using his immense strength, shape-shifting abilities, and strategic acumen to outmaneuver and defeat many of Tosakan's most feared champions. His feats include leaping over fortifications, burning down much of the city, engaging in fierce duels, subduing many formidable adversaries, and causing havoc throughout the enemy ranks.

At the same time Phra Ram led the battle from the front, demonstrating unwavering courage and wisdom while fighting alongside his troops like a true warrior-king. Armed with celestial weapons granted him by the gods, he confronted Tosakan's mightiest warriors, defeating them one by one. Phra Ram's prowess in archery, his strategic insights, and his inspirational leadership mobilized and inspired his forces toward victory.

The powerful Demon King Tosakan had ten faces and multiple arms, making him an intimidating opponent. He also possessed his own range of magical abilities and weapons bestowed upon him by the gods. Phra Ram, on the other hand, appeared as a human but was actually the avatar of Phra Narai. Therefore, he embodied the strength and intelligence of a god and was equipped with celestial weapons to aid him in battle. Their confrontation was intense and multifaceted, with both combatants employing a wide array of magical weapons and strategies. Phra Ram used his divine bow and arrows imbued with mystical powers. These weapons could target specific vulnerabilities of Tosakan, bypassing his magical defenses and causing significant damage. The gods played a crucial role in the duel as well, often intervening to aid Phra Ram or to ensure that the battle's outcome would align with the cosmic order and the restoration of Dharma.

The conflict reached its climax when Phra Ram, recognizing the need for a decisive blow, invoked a powerful divine weapon often described as an enchanted arrow, specifically created to defeat Tosakan. With the precise aim and the blessings of the gods, Phra Ram released the arrow, which found its mark, striking Tosakan a fatal blow. This brought an end to his rule in Lanka and ceased his tyranny over all the realms. After Tosakan's defeat, all the realms celebrated as Phra Ram's forces symbolized the triumph of good over evil. It marked the restoration of moral and cosmic order in the universe. Sida and Phra Ram were reunited and eventually returned to the kingdom of Ayutthaya. This restoration marked the beginning of a golden age, with Phra Ram's righteous rule heralding the return of the divine Dharma and a period of prosperity and justice.

The Ramakien has served as a source of divine inspiration for Thai monarchs, many of whom adopted titles and roles that mirror the epic's portrayal of righteous and godlike leadership. Through its intricate narrative and profound characters, it reflects the complexities of the human condition and the eternal quest for harmony and righteousness, themes that resonate deeply within Thai culture and spirituality.

Hanuman and Phra Ram's heroic feats, defined by precision, agility, strength, speed, and strategic brilliance, have also inspired generations of Muay Boran and Muay Thai warriors. Their exceptional abilities—mastery of aerial techniques, divine accuracy, and unwavering mental and physical resilience—continue to serve as a model for marital artists. Hanuman, in particular, embodies the ideals of courage, discipline, and loyalty, qualities deeply revered by fighters who strive to integrate the warrior's spirit with spiritual devotion both inside and outside the ring. His legacy transcends mere combat, representing the higher ideals of endurance, honor, and selflessness that resonate throughout Thai martial culture.

CHAPTER FOUR

ICONIC FIGURES IN THAI MARTIAL HISTORY

FINDING DIRECTION IN THE STORM

During my formative years, against a backdrop of personal struggles and intermittent education, martial arts became my sanctuary. As I tried to discover my cultural identity and grappled with the absence of my father, my mother became increasingly devoted to her Christian faith, which caused a distance between us. I lacked direction in my life, and I often felt unsure of what I could achieve in the world around me.

College life in London was a bit of a mixed bag for me. The business administration course I had chosen wasn't a great fit, though I enjoyed the social aspects of college. During this time, a friend invited me to a Muay Thai class, which became a new educational direction for me. The training was transformative: it was physically demanding and challenging, but also pushed me to break through limitations and awaken my warrior spirit.

My first Muay Thai teacher was Ralph Beale from Minotaur Thai Boxing Gym. Established in 1993 by Ralph Beale and Paul Taylor, the gym had a strong reputation for traditional techniques and rigorous training regimens producing skilled Muay Thai fighters. Ralph was an accomplished fighter and teacher with his dual Thai and British heritage. He became a pivotal figure in my martial arts journey by introducing me to the science and art of the eight limbs, and his dedication and skill inspired and motivated me.

For me Muay Thai training was more than just learning to fight; it was a profound journey of self-discovery. Each session enhanced my resilience and commitment. Despite the physical limitation of my hand, I adapted and excelled, finding the rigorous combination of punches, elbows, knees, and kicks a return to an innate part of myself. Developing myself as a Muay Thai warrior helped me to deal with the absence of my father by empowering my masculine energy, strengthening my physical body and mind, and providing a safe outlet for me to channel my pain and negative energy.

However, life outside my martial arts training was less straightforward. I was expelled from college abruptly when I was falsely accused of selling cannabis. My mother and I were at odds at the time as well, each seeking different directions in life. So at seventeen, I left home and became homeless for some time, staying with friends and eventually moving into the London hostel system.

All of this took me too far from Ralph to continue training with him. I next landed at Cobra Gym in Victoria. At the time, the gym was known for specializing in both Thai boxing and kickboxing under the guidance of Tim Izsly. It became the new home for my Muay Thai practice, offering a fresh environment to continue my training. Tim was a former champion with a no-nonsense approach. With him, I honed my skills further. The gym environment, though gritty, provided the perfect setting for me to flourish as a fighter, allowing me to build not only physical strength but also a deeper understanding of my capabilities. One day, a Japanese woman practicing yoga at the gym showed me how to do the crow pose. I realized for the first time that my arms couldn't stretch evenly after my childhood injury. That forced me to confront the full extent of my physical limitations, which I had managed to ignore up to that point, through sheer willpower.

This new insight marked a significant turning point in my life. After I decided to confront and overcome my physical restrictions, my training evolved to focus not only on martial skills but also on healing and realigning my body. This new phase of my martial arts journey became about fighting my own limitations, turning my training into a form of personal therapy.

KING SI INTHRATHIT:
THE BIRTH OF THE SUKHOTHAI KINGDOM

The legend of the Sukhothai Kingdom starts with Pho Khun Si Nao Nam Thom, the first ruler or chieftain of Sukhothai, founded in the 1200s. In Thai culture, founding figures like him are venerated for their foresight, leadership, and contributions to their communities. Although the historical records of his deeds are limited, oral traditions honor Pho Khun Si Nao Nam Thom for establishing Sukhothai, which would later become the cradle of Thai culture, Buddhism, and literature. However, during the early period of the Sukhothai Kingdom, the Thai people's spiritual beliefs were deeply influenced by a blend of animism, Buddhism, and Hindu mythology. The Thai people of this time had strong beliefs in the presence of protective spirits, ancestral veneration, and local deities connected to natural elements like water, mountains, and forests. These beliefs were integrated into their daily lives, agricultural practices, and governance. Pho

Khun Si Nao Nam Thom is described as a local leader who built Sukhothai into a flourishing town. Yet after his death, the city was vulnerable and eventually conquered and absorbed into the Khmer Empire.

Sometime later, frustrated by heavy taxes and foreign rule, another local chieftain from Bang Yang named Pho Khun Bang Klang Hao saw an opportunity to rebel as the Khmer Empire's focus on grand architectural projects had weakened its defenses. Pho Khun Bang Klang Hao allied with Khun Pha Mueang, the leader of Mueang Rat, and together they led a successful uprising. After liberating Si Satchanalai, Bang Klang Hao gave control of the town to Pha Mueang, who in return ceded the city of Sukhothai to him.

Bang Klang Hao was declared king of the newly independent Sukhothai Kingdom and given the regnal name and title of Si Inthrathit, derived from Sanskrit and meaning "The Revered Indra of the Sun," conveying to all that he ruled with divine authority, strength, and connection to both the god Indra and the power of the sun. This name reflected influences from Hindu traditions, associating the king with the head of the gods in Hindu mythology, a being symbolizing strength and divine protection.

Si Inthrathit's bravery and leadership also earned him the title Phra Ruang ("Glorious Prince"), which would lay the foundation of the Phra Ruang dynasty. His reign marked the establishment of the first true Thai kingdom and set the stage for the development of Thai culture, religion, and governance.

The adoption of Buddhism, particularly Theravada Buddhism, became more widespread under Si Inthrathit and his successors. While these Buddhist beliefs and traditions became dominant, the animistic and Hindu traditions and the belief in spirits and gods remained interwoven with religious practices. From the kingdom's inception, its rulers were seen as semidivine figures, often viewed as Dharmaraja—righteous rulers who governed according to Buddhist principles.

KING RAMATHIBODI: THE FOUNDER OF AYUTTHAYA

Ramathibodi I (1315–1369), originally known as Prince U Thong or "Golden Cradle," was the founder and first king of the Ayutthaya Kingdom, Siam's most powerful capital for more than four centuries. In Thai, *Rama* refers to the hero Pha Ram, an avatar of Vishnu from the Thai/Hindu epic Ramakien embodying righteousness and strength. *Thibodi*, from the Sanskrit *adhipati*, translates to "lord" or "ruler." Together, Ramathibodi essentially means "Lord Rama" or "Sovereign Lord." King Ramathibodi I's royal title highlighted his role as a just, powerful, and morally integral ruler, personifying qualities associated with the legendary hero Pha Ram. This title not only asserted his sovereignty but also connected his reign with a revered spiritual and moral legacy in Thai culture. It was a deliberate choice that linked him to a divine lineage, reinforcing that he ruled with both earthly and spiritual authority. In the later Chakri dynasty, the shortened form of this title, Rama, became the established convention for monarchs. This tradition has continued through ten reigns, from King Rama I to the present King Rama X.

Ramathibodi I was crowned on March 4, 1351, uniting the regions of Ayutthaya, Lop Buri, and Suphan Buri under his rule and establishing Ayutthaya as a dominant regional force. He maintained peace with the Sukhothai Kingdom to the north, concentrating his campaigns against the powerful Khmer Empire to eventually secure Ayutthaya's regional self-governance. His diplomatic and military pursuits and proactive approach to international trade elevated Ayutthaya to a vibrant commercial and cultural center.

Ramathibodi was also a devout Theravada Buddhist and declared it the kingdom's official religion, further unifying Ayutthaya's cultural identity. His reign marked the formation of the Siamese legal system rooted in Buddhist and Khmer values, which continued to guide Thai law for generations until the reign of Chulalongkorn in the nineteenth century.

KHUN PAEN:
A WARRIOR OF LEGEND AND MAGIC

Khun Paen is an iconic figure in Thai folklore, celebrated for his skill in combat, mastery of magic, and legendary charm. His story, rooted in oral tradition and later recorded in the Thai epic *Khun Chang Khun Paen*, unfolds in the Ayutthaya Kingdom's golden age of 1491–1529 under King Rama I and weaves a tale of loyalty, rivalry, love, and supernatural prowess.

Central to the story are three characters: Phlai Kaew, who later became known as Khun Paen; Nang Phim Philalai, who is also known as Wanthong; and Khun Chang, who grew up together with them in Suphanburi. Phlai Kaew, admired for his intelligence and charm, was raised with a strong sense of loyalty, while Nang Phim was known for her beauty. Khun Chang, though wealthy and well-connected, envied Phlai Kaew's appeal and kindness. The three shared a bond that later evolved into a love triangle, setting the stage for intense rivalry, romance, and betrayal. This early connection built the foundation for the complex, lifelong relationships that fueled the famous tale of *Khun Chang Khun Paen*.

Phlai Kaew was born in what is now central Thailand into a military family. From a young age, he was trained in horseback riding, archery, and martial arts, earning respect wherever he went. However, his father, a high-ranking officer, made a critical error in battle when Phlai Kaew was just ten, leading to his execution. This tragedy forced Phlai Kaew and his mother to flee to Kanchanaburi, where he began studying with monks at a nearby Buddhist monastery. Under the guidance of revered abbot Arjan Kong, Phlai Kaew learned Sanskrit, combat, and mystical arts. His training involved fearless nights in cemeteries to learn spirit control, which taught him to harness supernatural powers including protective spells and spirit manipulation.

Years later during the Songkran festival, Phlai Kaew, still a novice monk, was reunited with Wanthong when she offered him alms. Sparks flew as they rekindled their bond and transformed their childhood friendship into a deep romantic connection. Driven by this love, Phlai Kaew eventually left the monastic life to join the Ayutthaya military. He quickly rose through the ranks, demonstrating prowess in Muay Boran and Krabi-Krabong, and was awarded the noble title Khun Paen, signifying his status as a warrior of distinction. Alongside his combat skills, Khun Paen had developed supernatural abilities, such as invisibility, invincibility, and spirit-summoning, which set him apart as an unmatched warrior.

Khun Paen and Wanthong married, uniting their fates amid the complications of Khun Chang's persistent pursuit. Using his wealth and influence, Khun Chang manipulated circumstances to keep the two apart, even persuading the king to send Khun Paen on dangerous military campaigns. After years of fighting, Khun Paen returned home victorious, only to find that Khun Chang had falsely claimed he was dead and taken Wanthong as his own. In anger, Khun Paen abducted Wanthong, and they lived together in hiding.

On his next return from battle, Khun Paen brought home a second wife, Laothong, further straining his relationship with Wanthong. The move was motivated by his loyalty to the kingdom, as he had been rewarded with her by the king for his success in battle. Though his intent was rooted in duty, this deeply hurt Wanthong, who felt abandoned and betrayed. Disheartened, she eventually sought solace with Khun Chang, whose wealth and persistent devotion offered her stability and comfort. Khun Paen and Wanthong also had a son by this time, Phlai Ngam, conceived during one of the brief periods when they were together after Khun Paen had returned from battle.

Even though Wanthong was living with Khun Chang, he was still obsessed and deeply resentful of Khun Paen and so plotted to eliminate their son Phlai Ngam to sever Wanthong's last tie to her husband. When Phlai Ngam was eight, Khun Chang attempted to take his life under the guise of a family visit, but Phlai Ngam escaped to Kanchanaburi, where he found refuge with Khun Paen's mother. Under her guidance, Phlai Ngam grew up studying his father's military and mystical texts, eventually developing the resilience and skills needed to follow in his father's footsteps.

Khun Chang continued his scheming, accusing Khun Paen of disloyalty to the king. Arrested and stripped of his title, Khun Paen endured years of imprisonment while Khun Chang assumed control over Wanthong. Eventually, Phlai Ngam petitioned for his father's release as Khun Paen's military skills were urgently needed in Ayutthaya's war with Chiang Mai. Together, Khun Paen and Phlai Ngam led a successful campaign, capturing the king of Chiang Mai and thereby restoring Khun Paen's reputation. He was appointed governor of Kanchanaburi, and Phlai Ngam earned the honor of serving in the royal pages.

The tragic climax of Khun Paen's story unfolded when Wanthong was brought before the king and forced to choose between Khun Paen and Khun Chang. Unable to decide, she remained silent, leading the king to order her execution. Phlai Ngam's plea for mercy arrived too late, sealing Wanthong's fate and the tragic end of their love story.

After Wanthong's execution, Khun Paen continued his life as a warrior, serving the king in legendary battles and developing his own supernatural abilities. He eventually took another wife, Nang Buaklee. However, due to conflicts between him and the ruling authorities, Nag Buaklee was taken from him while pregnant with their son. She was forced to live under the control of another lord but, fearing that the child would grow up to become a challenge to the ruling elite, she was executed before the child was born. After learning of Nang Buaklee's and his child's death, Khun Paen retrieved the unborn fetus of their child and performed a sinister but power magical ritual.

Through the ritual, Khun Paen bound the spirit of his unborn son to serve as his Kuman Thong, a protective guardian, capable of warning him of danger, protecting him in battle, and offering supernatural support. The Kuman Thong became a symbol of loyalty, protection, and resilience.

Today, Khun Paen's legacy as a warrior-mystic endures. His amulets are popular among fighters and spiritual practitioners, offering strength, protection, and charisma. The legend of Khun Paen, master of both martial and mystical arts, celebrates bravery, resilience, and the profound influence of a hero who rose from humble beginnings to become an enduring icon of Thai culture.

BATTLES FOR AYUTTHAYA: KING NARESUAN'S STRATEGIC STRIKE

During the Burmese-Siamese War of 1563–64 under King Maha Chakkraphat, Ayutthaya faced a series of invasions from the Burmese. In a strategic move during one of these sieges, young Prince Naresuan was taken to Burma as a royal hostage and raised in a foreign kingdom. During his time in captivity, he learned Burmese and Siamese martial arts, as the Burmese court trained him as both a potential ruler and a warrior. This experience exposed him to Burmese martial techniques while solidifying his resolve to free Siam from Burmese control. He gained considerable experience in statecraft and warfare, leaving him a skilled warrior and a tactical leader.

Prince Naresuan was released from captivity in Burma due to a change in political circumstances following the death of the Burmese king Bayinnaung in 1581. Bayinnaung's successor, King Nanda Bayin, faced several internal and external challenges, including rebellions and political instability within the Burmese Empire.

After his return to Ayutthaya, Prince Naresuan eventually ascended to the throne. Back in Siam, King Naresuan continued his training under Siamese martial art masters, experts in both close-combat techniques such as strikes, clinching, and grappling and weapons training with swords, staffs, shields, and spears, preparing him for melees and ranged engagements on the battlefield. His experience and the skills acquired during his captivity helped him lead successful military campaigns against Burma, contributing significantly to the independence and consolidation of the Siamese Kingdom. Naresuan's release and subsequent actions played a crucial role in shaping the history of Thailand, and he is celebrated as a national hero for his efforts in thwarting Burmese domination.

In 1593, the Burmese forces led by Crown Prince Mingyi Swa advanced into Siamese territory near Suphanburi. During the battle, with both armies engaged, a duel unfolded between King Naresuan of Ayutthaya and Crown Prince Mingyi Swa of Burma. Mounted on their war elephants and with their elite warrior guards in attendance, the king and crown prince faced each other. This was more than a clash of swords; it was a symbolic fight for dominance and the freedom it would bring. The battlefield was charged with tension as the elephants and their riders clashed violently, King Naresuan and Crown Prince Mingyi Swa exchanging ferocious blows with spears. On the ground, King Naresuan's Lang Muay guards engaged in fierce combat with the soldiers of Prince Mingyi Swa. In a pivotal moment marked by exceptional skill and bravery, King Naresuan delivered a decisive, fatal blow against the Burmese prince. The death of Prince Mingyi Swa devastated the morale of the Burmese troops, triggering their eventual retreat and defeat.

This momentous victory at Suphanburi not only secured Ayutthaya's independence but also solidified King Naresuan's status as a revered national hero. His strategic foresight, valor in the face of overwhelming odds, and dedication to his kingdom's sovereignty have become emblematic of Thailand's national character, celebrated and honored for generations.

The development of ancient Siamese fighting systems, now known as Muay Boran, began to gain recognition around 1584, during the reign of King Naresuan. Renowned for his combat skills, King Naresuan regarded martial arts training as essential for his soldiers, encouraging the rigorous practice of Muay techniques and self-defense skills within his ranks. His deep personal interest in the art greatly boosted its popularity.

As Muay spread beyond the military to the general public, civilians began practicing and adapting the techniques they observed, leading to the evolution of new fighting styles and strategies. This period laid the foundation for organized fighting events, transforming Muay from a strictly military discipline into a cultural sport and setting the stage for formalized bouts and competitions.

THE UNCONQUERED SPIRIT: THE TIGER KING

In 1661, an unofficial prince was born in the Phichit province of Ayutthaya. He was the secret son of King Narai and his concubine Princess Kusawadi of Chiang Mai. He was given the title of Luang Sorasak, which can be interpreted to mean someone of high standing with a reputation for virtue and strength. As the unofficial son of the king, he was adopted out to Phetracha, the founder of the Ban Phlu Luang dynasty. Phetracha was a prominent figure in the Ayutthaya Kingdom, who would later become king himself.

As the child of Phetracha, Luang Sorasak was still groomed for a significant role in the kingdom, receiving education and training befitting a member of the royal family. Guided by the esteemed martial master Ajahn Saeng, the young Luang Sorasak would have received rigorous training in the martial disciplines essential for maintaining power and stability in the Ayutthaya Kingdom. This training included not only physical combat but also strategies for leadership and governance. Ajahn Saeng was a highly respected figure known for his expertise in martial arts and military strategy during the Ayutthaya period. His guidance would have been crucial in preparing Luang Sorasak for leadership and the responsibilities of ruling a kingdom.

Many details of Luang Sorasak's early life are missing along with the lost records from the Ayutthaya period. However, it is speculated that the youth was very interested in learning the fighting art of the eight limbs, later known as Muay Thai. He was reportedly involved in various clashes and brawls. This was not uncommon for young nobles of the time, as martial prowess was highly valued and often tested in real combat situations. His participation in these incidents would have contributed to his physical and tactical skills, enhancing his reputation and competence in martial arts.

His ascension to the throne was not just a political transition but also entangled with his own complex legacy. Following the death of his true father King Narai, and the subsequent death of the next king, his adoptive father Phetracha, he then had to contend with his younger half brother Prince Khwan for the kingship.

In 1703, Luang Sorasak emerged victorious. He was crowned King Somdet Phra Sanphet VIII or King Suriyenthrathibodi, with the latter meaning the "Bearer of the Sun's Wisdom." However, his reign as the twenty-ninth monarch of Ayutthaya was marred by allegations of cruelty and moral corruption.

More interesting than his official duties was how he comported himself personally. Not one to be caged by the trappings of palace life or his royal station, he regularly ventured forth from his palace, delighting in fishing, hunting, fighting in the ring, and indulging in the pleasures of the flesh. According to legend, no one dared to fight him in the ring as king, so he began to disguise himself as a commoner and entered local fights and tournaments, weaving through the crowds an anonymous warrior among many. In these arenas, he fought as simply a man among men. With victory after victory, he proved his might, his skill transcending the gap between the throne and earth. He was known for his fierce fighting spirit and style, emphasizing forceful attacks that made his technique more aggressive and direct than defensive strategies, focusing on inflicting maximum damage quickly.

It's during one these instances, as the story goes, that the Siamese commoners gave him the acclaimed nickname "Phra Chao Sua"—"The Tiger King." This name was supposedly a reference to his ferocity in the ring as well as his larger-than-life character.

He was also known for his extravagant and flamboyant lifestyle. It is said that he enjoyed grand ceremonies and luxurious displays, which were highly unusual and dramatic compared to other monarchs of the time. It was also recorded that his passion for hunting, particularly for tigers, was legendary, which contributed to the nickname.

His reign continued to support the popularity of Muay Boran not only as a combat practice for soldiers but also as a national sport and form of entertainment. This period laid crucial groundwork for Muay Boran to be codified, shaping the techniques, traditions, and ritualistic aspects we see today in modern Muay Thai. While there isn't a single manuscript solely dedicated to detailing the Tiger King's fighting style, royal records, historical chronicles, and the oral history passed down by Muay Thai masters reference his techniques and influence. These sources recount that King Phra Chao Sua was an avid practitioner of Muay Boran and was personally trained in the art, emphasizing techniques in unarmed and armed combat. He is believed to have favored an aggressive fighting style, employing powerful strikes and close combat techniques. These qualities align closely with the Muay Chaiya and Muay Korat styles, known for their strong, grounded stances and the effective use of elbows and knees for swift, impactful attacks.

However, his personal tale is juxtaposed with darker aspects of his rule, particularly highlighted in the Chronicle of Ayutthaya (Phan Chanthanumat version), which portrays him as a ruler who engaged in acts of cruelty. He is depicted as leveraging his power for immoral purposes, especially in his treatment of women and those who defied him. These accounts reveal a complex and flawed character, whose darker traits starkly contrast with his contributions to martial arts and the cultural heritage of Muay Thai. His story serves as a cautionary tale, reminding us of how martial prowess intertwined with unchecked power can corrupt, illustrating the complex interplay between human greatness and flawed vices.

In 1708, amid a tumultuous political climate, the Tiger King was dethroned by another of his brothers, King Borommakotin, in a significant moment in the history of the Ayutthaya Kingdom. This deposition was the culmination of a long-standing rivalry and political struggle between the two. The Tiger King would die in exile, though the exact details of his death are not extensively documented.

Tales of the Tiger King's incognito fighting victories have become embedded in Thai historical legend and folklore. His contributions to Muay Thai are commemorated annually on National Muay Thai Day, celebrated on February 6 in honor of King Sanphet VIII. The Tiger King's distinctive style influenced regional Muay Boran systems and became foundational to Muay Thai's progression, where his techniques evolved to suit both battlefield combat and competitive arenas.

Triumph in Defeat: The Victories of Nai Khanomtom

For over four centuries, from 1351 to 1767, the kingdom of Ayutthaya's formidable walls and defenses repelled numerous assaults and preserved its sovereignty against various aggressors. However, in 1767, the kingdom faced an unprecedented threat when Burmese forces armed with refined tactics and hardened by years of combat experience, especially against the Siamese kingdoms, focused their attention on Ayutthaya. They launched a determined and strategically planned assault aimed at finally breaching Ayutthaya's defenses and subjugating the kingdom.

For months, the mighty Burmese army laid siege, a relentless assault that drained the city's resources and the spirit of the people. The defenders fought tirelessly to repel the unyielding

Burmese onslaught but with no success. As the siege continued, the defenders and people of the kingdom lost heart and the tides of fortune began to turn against them. The once impregnable walls of Ayutthaya, which had stood as proud guardians of the kingdom for hundreds of years, were finally breached.

The prolonged siege had left the inhabitants of Ayutthaya in a dire state, plagued by hunger and despair. When the city's defenses eventually crumbled, the Burmese embarked on a devastating campaign of looting and burning, turning majestic temples into hollow shells and priceless works of art into mere fragments of their former glory. The once vibrant kingdom of Ayutthaya, a beacon of knowledge, culture, and trade, was reduced to smoldering ruins. Its libraries, brimming with centuries of accumulated wisdom and heritage, were mercilessly destroyed, an incalculable loss of Thai history and culture.

The invaders spared few, as soldiers and civilians alike fell victim to the onslaught. Those who did survive the sword faced an equally grim fate—bound in chains as slaves or prisoners of war. A wide cross section of the population was taken captive, from nobles and skilled artisans to commoners and warriors, all relocated to Burma. Many became laborers helping to build Burmese cities like Ava. Skilled artisans, craftsmen, and scholars were often employed in their respective fields to enhance Burmese culture and technology. Some of the captured were incorporated into the Burmese military. A notable warrior named Nai Khanomtom was one of those taken prisoner. His story is regarded in Thai history as an expression of the resilience and the enduring spirit of Siamese people in the face of overwhelming adversity.

Legend has it that Nai Khanomtom was already renowned in his homeland for his exceptional combat skills, but now he was defeated, shackled, and transported to Burma. To celebrate the Burmese New Year, King Hsinbyushin organized a festival and a series of martial arts competitions to celebrate his kingdom's rise to power. The king wanted to prove that the Burmese style was superior and called for the best Siamese warriors alive to fight his warriors.

The Burmese system was known as Banshay, a weapon-based martial art that employed swords, staffs, spears, and hand-to-hand combat, similar to Muay Boran. In modern times, Banshay has evolved into a primarily hand-to-hand combat system and is now commonly referred to as Lethwei. It emphasizes strikes using fists, legs, elbows, knees, and head but also incorporates throws and grappling techniques.

During the Burmese games, many Siamese warriors were killed in combat, providing grim entertainment as the Burmese repeatedly celebrated their victories. Among those set to fight was Nai Khanomtom, known for his formidable skills. His reputation had sparked the interest of the Burmese king, who ordered that Nai Khanomtom be matched against a famous Burmese champion to test his abilities.

As the day of the fight dawned, a multitude of spectators gathered, buzzing with excitement. Before the match began, Nai Khanomtom performed the sacred Ram Muay and Wai Kru rituals honoring his teachers, family, and spiritual traditions. This unusual spectacle puzzled and captivated the Burmese audience, who had never before witnessed such a display.

The environment of this ancient battle was starkly different from today's combat sports. There were no rounds, no timekeepers, and no referees. Fighters did not wear gloves; instead, their hands were wrapped in hemp ropes. The match was not intended to be fair but a brutal contest to the finish, where eye gouging, groin strikes, bone breaks, and lethal moves were all legitimate tactics. This bare-knuckle death match unfolded not in a ring but in an arena, set against the backdrop of a triumphant Burmese court and surrounded by crowds of commoners thirsting for spectacle, reminiscent of the gladiatorial arenas of ancient Rome. As the fight commenced, Nai Khanomtom's superior Muay Boran skills were immediately evident. When the Burmese champion launched a furious combination of punches, Nai Khanomtom easily blocked and evaded them while swiftly counterattacking with a devastating barrage of punches, elbows, knees, and kicks. Employing close-range clinch techniques and a decisive throw, he swiftly ended the bout. He used his tactical prowess and overwhelming force to subdue the Burmese champion, securing himself a swift and decisive victory. The crowd was stunned and left in silence, shocked by the ease with which their celebrated champion was defeated.

However, King Hsinbyushin was unconvinced by this single fight and ordered Nai Khanomtom to face nine more Burmese champions in succession. Nai Khanomtom rose to the challenge and proceeded to take down each one, showcasing extraordinary endurance, resilience, and the remarkable skill of a Siamese warrior.

The differences in fighting styles were stark. Burmese boxers, dressed in traditional ankle-length sarongs, moved slowly, circling their opponents and cautiously searching for openings. In contrast, Siamese fighters wore a loincloth, knotted at the back, which afforded them greater freedom and mobility. Nai Khanomtom employed a dynamic array of techniques, utilizing all nine limbs—fists, elbows, knees, shins, and headbutts—coupled with advanced clinching tactics. His approach was to adapt in the moment, countering each opponent's strengths and exploiting their weaknesses with precise, powerful strikes and strategic clinches. This versatile and agile fighting style gave him a clear tactical edge over the Burmese contenders. One after another, the Burmese champions fell. The king watched in awe as Nai Khanomtom dominated the arena.

Impressed by his unmatched skills and the grace with which he executed each move, the king granted Nai Khanomtom his freedom. From that moment on, Nai Khanomtom's renown grew not just as a symbol of Thai resistance and resilience but as the very embodiment of Muay Boran and Muay Thai. He became an enduring symbol, celebrated annually on March 17 as National Muay Thai Day in Thailand, forever immortalized as the "Father of Muay Thai."

It is also said that during the fall of Ayutthaya, the biography of Khun Paen, the renowned Siamese warrior from the kingdom's golden age, was recorded by Thai prisoners in Burma. Over time, the details of his story continued to evolve, gaining embellishments and becoming more richly woven into Thai folklore. This evolving narrative has made Khun Paen's legacy not only a historical account but a blend of myth and cultural symbolism that resonates deeply in Thai history and spirituality.

CHAPTER FIVE

TRADITIONS OF ANCIENT WARFARE

FISTS AND FORTITUDE

At twenty-one, I suffered a dislocated hip from a bad fall, a painful incident that misaligned my hip and triggered a cascade of new physical issues. This injury didn't just bring physical pain; it forced me to make serious changes. I took it as a sign from the universe to focus on healing my physical imbalances and finding greater meaning in my life. In this period of introspection, a quote from a Spider-Man film struck a chord with me: "It's not only the friendships you make that define you but also the ones you break." This realization propelled me to sever ties with people who didn't have my best interests at heart, although it meant walking a more solitary path. This decision marked the beginning of a transformative journey of self-discovery for me that mirrored the life of a monk withdrawing from the world to seek wisdom in solitude.

I delved into books on personal development; African, Caribbean, and world history; psychology; and spirituality. I embraced a disciplined lifestyle, avoiding meat, alcohol, and other indulgences to focus instead on training, study, and personal growth. I persisted with self-led rehabilitation, working intensively on my physical alignment, breaking down scar tissue in my wrist from my old hand injury, and strengthening my hip and my core through targeted exercises. This ongoing effort was crucial not only for my physical health but also for my psychological well-being.

My martial arts then led me to All Stars Boxing Gym, a welcoming space not far from my home in West London. This gym, established by Ghanaian boxing champion Mr. Akay, fostered a positive environment for aspiring boxers. Every Saturday it offered Muay Thai classes run by a great team of coaches: Mick, Del, Lloyd, and Shaz were all highly skilled and passionate about both training in boxing and Muay Thai and teaching others. Here the coaches and fellow martial artists all shared their knowledge generously, helping me to refine my skills in Muay Thai and boxing. The positive atmosphere and communal spirit of the gym played a significant role in my recovery and growth.

While training at All Stars one day, I had the opportunity to spar with an older London-born Nigerian warrior named RA. The coaches called us into the ring to face each other. After we touched gloves and began sparring, RA unleashed a barrage of powerful punches and kicks. I skillfully blocked and evaded his strikes, countering with my own punches and leg kicks. While he managed to block some of my kicks, others landed effectively. This exchange fueled his determination, and he responded with a flurry of combinations. Our match was hard-fought and ended with a more or less even outcome. Afterward, we both acknowledged each other's skills and unwavering fighting spirit. We formed a friendship, and RA not only pushed me both physically and mentally, but he also highlighted for me a holistic view of martial arts. Through him, I discovered how to balance the knowledge of how to kill in combat with the wisdom of how to heal myself and others.

Over time and with consistent effort, I improved the alignment and control of my fingers, wrists, elbows, shoulders, hip, and legs. I was far from healed, but I was gradually making progress. The process involved mobility exercises, stretching, cracking and clicking parts of my body back into alignment, while breaking down scar tissue and softening fascia. In my quest for healing, I received acupuncture and massage treatments from practitioners of Traditional Chinese Medicine as well as Thai massage. I explored other practices like tai chi and qigong, both of which significantly enhanced my mobility and alignment, elevated the fluidity of my movements, deepened my connection to my life force, and sharpened my control over my breath. My fighting endurance improved because I could breathe better, and the flow and control of my Muay Thai combinations also improved.

Muay Boran: The Source of Nine Limbs

Muay Boran is not a single unified fighting system; rather, it is a modern umbrella term that encompasses a collection of regional styles of Thai hand-to-hand combat, each shaped by different influences and adapted to local environments and cultural needs. The term *Muay* simply means "boxing" in Thai and has been used broadly for centuries to refer to Thai fighting arts. The name *Muay Boran* literally translates to "ancient boxing" and refers to the historical range of fighting techniques used for self-protection, combat, and military training. These regional styles each had distinctions but also shared a similarity and made use of nine natural weapons: two hands, two elbows, two knees, two legs (shins and feet), and the head.

After years of rigorous training, the ancient Siamese warriors known as Nak Muay would condition their bodies into formidable weapons. Each Muay Boran style contributed to this transformation, honing their knuckles, elbows, knees, shins, and head and turning each into powerful tools for both attack and defense. Through this intense physical conditioning, these warriors mastered the art of striking and defending with the hardest parts of their bodies, making them as effective as traditional weapons like swords, axes, spears, and shields.

As mentioned in the intro, the origins of Muay Thai are shrouded in mystery, woven with myths, legends, and conflicting historical accounts. Some traditions trace its roots back to the early days of the Thai people, with one of the oldest accounts dating as far back as 657 C.E. According to legend, a wise hermit named Sukatanta established a martial arts school in Lopburi that taught techniques resembling what we now call Muay Boran and Muay Thai, laying the foundation for this revered fighting system. However, the true development of Thai fighting systems can be seen more clearly in later periods. During the Sukhothai Kingdom (thirteenth through fourteenth century), Muay was a vital tool for liberation, helping the Siamese people resist and eventually break free from the control of the Khmer Empire. This tradition of martial resistance continued into the Ayutthaya period (fourteenth through eighteenth century), where Muay Boran played a crucial role in the eventual defeat of the Khmer and the establishment of Ayutthaya as the dominant power in the region. From its earliest days, Muay Boran was not just a martial art but a highly effective combat system that was taught and practiced by ordinary people—warriors, monks, and royalty alike—all of whom contributed to the defense and protection of their kingdom. It has remained a defining element of Siamese, and later Thai, culture, shaping both the nation's identity and its military success.

In 1909, during the reign of King Chulalongkorn (Rama V), an important event took place that marked the formal recognition of regional styles. The king, a great patron of Thai culture and tradition, invited the governors from different regions of their kingdom, including, Korat, Chaiya, and Lopburi to bring their finest fighters to compete in a series of matches in honor of his son's funeral. This royal event was not just a display of physical prowess but a testament to the warrior spirit of the Thai people, especially at a time when the kingdom sought to preserve its cultural heritage amid growing Western influences.

From Korat, Chaiya, and Lopburi came three warriors who would rise to prominence for their exceptional skill. The matches held at the royal court were a test not only of strength and technique but of the distinct martial traditions each fighter carried with them. The fighter from Korat, known for his powerful, forceful punches, dominated his opponents with sheer aggression. The fighter from Chaiya, in contrast, demonstrated a graceful and balanced style, relying on posture, defense, and precision. The fighter from Lopburi was strategic and sharp, known for his wit and the precision of his strikes, effortlessly landing well-timed punches that cut through his opponent's defenses.

King Chulalongkorn, impressed by their mastery, awarded each fighter the prestigious title of Muen or "the King's Champion," an honor akin to knighthood in Western traditions. The Korat fighter was given the title Muen Changat Choeng Chok (Master of Skilled Combat), the Chaiya fighter was named Muen Muay Michue (Master of Elegant Boxing), and the Lopburi fighter became Muen Mae Mahd (Master of Precise Punches). These titles cemented for them a responsibility to preserve and teach their regional styles, ensuring the continuation of these unique traditions.

With this royal recognition, the three fighters returned to their regions to establish Muay Boran training camps and pass down their methods to future generations. Over time, as Muay Boran continued to evolve, a fourth regional style was added: Muay Tha Sao, known for its speed and agility. With the growing awareness of the distinct strengths of these regional styles, their characters became encapsulated in the descriptive names of Hard Punch Korat, Clever Lopburi, Posture Chaiya, Faster Tha Sao. Each phrase distilled the essence of the styles, highlighting the power-based techniques of Muay Korat, the strategic precision of Muay Lopburi, the defensive posture and timing of Muay Chaiya, and the speed and decisiveness of Muay Tha Sao.

While these four styles became the most recognized as reflecting the unique geography and combat needs of a given region, many other local variations of Muay existed throughout Thailand. The term Muay Boran grew into a way to refer to all these traditional forms of Muay existing prior to the sport's modernization into Muay Thai. As time passed and the art modernized and coalesced into Muay Thai, many of these regional styles were lost, preserved only in memory and local traditions. The remaining styles continued to develop their own distinct terminologies, principles, stances, and methods of training, even down to the unique patterns of rope wrapping that fighters would use to protect their hands.

Though the finer details of these historical events are difficult to verify in formal academic records, this narrative has endured in the oral tradition and continues to inform the way Muay Boran is taught and practiced around the world.

As described by the Italian grand master of Muay Boran Arjan Marco De Cesaris (whom I've had the pleasure of training with during one of his Hanuman workshops), the ancient Siamese fighting traditions can be broadly understood through two primary stylistic approaches that coexisted within Muay Boran: Muay Lak, the rooted (hard) style, and Muay Kiao, the pliable (soft) style. Muay Lak focuses on power, stability, and strength, where fighters maintain a solid, grounded stance to deliver forceful strikes. It is characterized by direct, heavy attacks and a strong, unwavering defense, designed to overwhelm opponents through sheer force. In contrast, Muay Kiao is more fluid and flexible, relying on agility, speed, and evasive movements. Fighters who use this style employ swift footwork and defensive techniques to dodge or neutralize an opponent's strikes, focusing on well-timed counterattacks and precision rather than brute force. Both styles offer different pathways to success in combat, with Muay Lak valuing raw power and Muay Kiao emphasizing agility and strategy.

Each regional style of Muay Boran embodies the broader principles of Muay Lak (the rooted and hard style) and Muay Kiao (the pliable and soft style) with local environments and needs shaping combat philosophies.

Regional Styles Associated with Muay Lak
(Rooted/Hard Style)

Muay Korat is a northeastern regional style that focuses on strength and power. It is known for its emphasis on forceful strikes, especially wide-swinging punches known as Mahd Wiang Kwai or "Throwing the Buffalo" most feared for their devastating power intended to knock out opponents with a single blow. The fighters in Muay Korat prioritize staying rooted and using a strong guard to defend while delivering devastating attacks.

The first patriarch of Muay Korat was Phra Hensamahan, the governor of Korat province. A scholar and martial artist, Phra Hensamahan authored textbooks on Muay and is credited with developing the most structured and coherent form of Muay Korat, much of which is still practiced today. He organized the techniques of Muay Korat around the concept of the 47 Portals, which include:

- 10 basic systems for utilizing the body's main weapons
- 5 fundamental combat strategies
- 11 methods for solving common problems encountered in a fight
- 21 ancient combat skills

This comprehensive system laid the foundation for Muay Korat's enduring legacy as a powerful and effective martial art. Another prominent figure in Muay Korat—taught by Phra Hensamahan—was Kruu Bua, considered the true master of the Muay Korat system. Kruu Bua, whose real name was Kruu Bua Ninarcha (meaning "The Black Horse"), dedicated his life to the art. After becoming a soldier, he spent his career passing down the traditions and techniques of Muay Korat to cadets in the Thai Army. Known as the Muay Thai of the East, Muay Korat emphasizes power, strikes, and forward movement, and Kruu Bua played a key role in preserving and advancing this style.

Muay Lopburi, originating from the central province of Lopburi, is a dynamic martial art heavily inspired by the movements of animals, such as elephants and monkeys, and mythical creatures and divine beings from the Ramakien. This style emphasizes agility, feints, and unpredictability, with a notable focus on jumping attacks. Muay Lopburi encompasses 16 Mae Mai (master techniques), and one of its distinctive features is a stance with palms facing upward, designed to maximize the effectiveness of its signature weapon: the uppercut punch known as Mahd Seuy. Muay Lopburi is often described as a "wise" or "clever" style because of its versatility, combining agility with precision.

The city of Lopburi, one of Thailand's oldest urban centers, is located about 150 kilometers (93 miles) northeast of Bangkok. According to legend, its origins are linked to the Ramakien. After

Pha Ram's victory over Tosakan, he shot an arrow to mark the site for a new settlement. His general, the divine monkey king Hanuman, followed this arrow and used the soil it landed in to build the city's walls, while Pha Ram created the city itself with his powers as an incarnation of Vishnu. The name Lopburi and the city's founding are memorialized by the Lopburi City Pillar Shrine (Son Pha Ram), believed to be Pha Ram's arrow turned to stone. Hanuman's role in the city's creation reflects Lopburi's strong connection to monkeys as a key cultural and spiritual symbol.

Muay Lopburi's unique techniques and strategies align with this mythical heritage. According to legend, Muay Lopburi is one of the oldest Muay Boran styles, with over a thousand years of history. It is said to have been developed in 675 by the mystical hermit Sukatanta of the Khao Samor Khon Martial Art School in Lopburi. The last student to have trained at this school was King Ramkhamhaeng of the Sukhothai Kingdom (736–755). However, it wasn't until around 600 years later that Muay Lopburi truly became an established style. Another monarch who practiced this boxing style was King Khun Ngam Muang, who ruled another Thai kingdom called Phayao from 1258 to 1298.

Muay Lopburi is believed to have been further developed during the Ayutthaya period, particularly during the reign of King Narai (1656–1688). At this time, the king's court saw an influx of foreign influences, as many outsiders were working with the king and his military. It is believed that Arjan Muun Men Mat, a renowned Muay Lopburi master, may have learned techniques from these foreign soldiers, further refining and developing certain aspects of the Muay Lopburi arsenal.

Scholars often debate whether Muay Lopburi belongs to the Muay Lak (rooted and hard style) or Muay Kiao (soft and pliable style) category. Muay Lopburi combines elements of both:

it incorporates the power and forward pressure characteristic of Muay Lak but also features the sophisticated defense and sharp counterattacks typical of Muay Kiao. This versatility allows Muay Lopburi to adapt to various body types and fighting styles. Fighters use a solid stance and calculated power strikes, particularly punches aimed at exploiting an opponent's weaknesses while maintaining flexible footwork that enables quick adjustments during combat. The typical stance of Muay Lopburi closely resembles that of a Western boxer from the early 1900s, with an upright posture, both arms extended outward, and forearms pointing forward. This stance supports the style's emphasis on precise and deadly punches, making it a highly effective striking system.

Regional Styles Associated with Muay Kiao (Pliable/Soft Style)

Muay Chaiya is one of the most renowned styles of Muay Boran, originating from the Chaiya district in Surat Thani province of Southern Thailand. This style is celebrated for its unique emphasis on defense, strength, balance, agility, and close-quarter combat. Fighters in Muay Chaiya adopt a low, compact stance to protect vital areas and excel in counterattacks, using their opponent's momentum against them and delivering sharp, precise strikes. The style's defensive focus and adaptability make it a highly respected and enduring element of Muay Boran.

The origins of Muay Chaiya are somewhat obscured by legend, but it is widely attributed to a fighter who became a revered Buddhist monk known for his dedication to both spiritual and physical training. The name of the fighter monk from Bangkok has never been officially documented, but locals chose to call him Poh Than Ma, "the Reverend Father Who Arrived at this Land."

According to tradition, Poh Than Ma traveled south to Chaiya after growing disillusioned with the bureaucracy in Bangkok. Upon reaching Tambon Phumriang, he earned local admiration when he reportedly caught a mischievous elephant using coconut shells. Impressed, the villagers built a monastery in his honor, naming it Wat Thoong Jub Chang (Temple of the Elephant Catching Field).

Muay Chaiya reflects the region's challenging terrain, emphasizing evasion, clever positioning, and counterattacks. Fighters are trained to absorb or deflect attacks before striking back with precision. Passed down through a lineage of dedicated teachers and students, Muay Chaiya remains one of the most versatile and well-rounded systems within Muay Boran, combining strength, technique, and adaptability in a way that has kept it relevant and respected for generations.

The defining qualities of Muay Chaiya are a practitioner's complete awareness and control over every movement, whether it's lifting the leg, positioning the arm, or wrapping the fist. Every action has a purpose, and each must be executed with precision. Muay Chaiya fighters are known for their focus, determination, and patience, training rigorously to master not only their techniques but also their emotions.

A key characteristic of Muay Chaiya is its strong, adaptable stance combined with protective hand positioning for a tight defense, ensuring that the fighter is protected from head to toe. Once a fighter can adequately defend themself, they rely on timing and opportunity to strike back with precision, hitting hard and fast. One of the most famous footwork techniques in Muay Chaiya is the Yang Sam Khum (Three-Step Approach), which allows fighters to attack and defend fluidly. This zigzag positioning of the feet in a triangular or three-point pattern enables quick changes in direction.

Muay Chaiya's mindful awareness, tight defense, timely strikes, and fluid footwork make the system a unique and adaptable martial art, ensuring its fighters are always in control both mentally and physically.

Muay Tha Sao is the last of the four main styles of Muay Boran and originates from the northern region of Thailand, particularly in the Tha Sao district. Known for its emphasis on speed, agility, and rapid footwork, this style was developed in an environment that demanded quick movements and precise strikes. Often referred to as "fast boxing," Muay Tha Sao is characterized by its nimble and decisive techniques, allowing practitioners to out-maneuver their opponents. It is an ideal style for fighters who prioritize speed and adaptability over brute strength, relying on fluid combinations and evasive maneuvers to control the fight.

Muay Tha Sao is believed to have originated during the Ayutthaya period (1350–1767) in the province of Uttaradit and is attributed to the teachings of Kru Mek, an acclaimed box-ing teacher of the time. Among his most famous students was Thongdee Funkhao, better known as Phraya Pichai of the Bro-ken Sword, who served as King Taksin's bodyguard. Phraya Pichai became a key figure in the development of the style, com-bining Muay Tha Sao with elements of Chinese boxing and sword fighting, eventually creating Muay Phraya Pichai, known for its distinctive and powerful boxing techniques.

Muay Tha Sao warriors are renowned for their stealthy yet powerful strikes, often likened to the swift, forceful blow of an ax. They are also celebrated for their flexibility and lightning-fast legwork, with kicks that "move like a whip," striking from all angles and at any height with precision and speed.

Guided by a deep understanding of physiology, Muay Tha Sao practitioners are taught to focus on how to effectively deliver each punch and kick to target critical areas of the body. This reflects the belief that Muay Tha Sao is not just a sport, but a real form of combat. The style's philosophy emphasizes that every strike must have a clear and purposeful intent, aiming for an efficient victory. Each movement is designed to serve a true combat purpose, embodying a practical approach to self-defense and offense.

The combination of speed, agility, and purposefully applied technique makes Muay Tha Sao one of the most enigmatic and highly respected Muay Boran styles, designed for those who seek to outpace and outmaneuver their opponents.

Among these regional Muay Boran styles, Muay Korat of the northeast is known for its raw power, Muay Lopburi of the central region for its precision, Muay Chaiya of the south for its defensive and counterattack mastery, and Muay Tha Sao of the north for its speed. Over time, these distinct styles have influenced various hybrid specialized systems, each with unique characteristics.

Some combined styles include the Muay Lung (Royal Style), a refined and specialized system designed for elite warriors tasked with protecting the monarchy. It incorporates the best techniques from all major styles, emphasizing strategy, direct attack, adaptability, defense, counterattack, and complete efficiency in combat. Another style is Muay Sua (Tiger King Style), a fierce and aggressive style that blends powerful, hard strikes with agility and relentless attacks. Then there is Muay Lert Rit, which is a modern military-oriented system that focuses on tactical efficiency, devasting close-range strikes, and survival-based techniques designed for real-life situations.

In the modern sense, Muay Boran can also be observed in two other distinct classifications: Pure Traditional and Evolved Forms. The Pure Traditional Muay Boran focuses on preserving the ancient Siamese techniques, rituals, and philosophies in their original form, emphasizing the cultural and spiritual elements passed down through generations. In contrast, the Evolved Form, while rooted in these traditions, incorporates influences from other martial arts, such as other Asian fighting systems and Western boxing, adapting and improving the techniques for modern combat and competition. This dual classification allows Muay Boran to be both a preserved cultural heritage and a dynamic, evolving martial art.

Each of these advanced and thorough Muay Boran systems integrates aspects of Buddhist principles such as mental discipline, mindfulness, and humility, as well as blending technical mastery with spiritual rituals like the Wai Khru and Ram Muay, expressed with regional and cultural differences. These traditions emphasize the importance of mental clarity, respect for teachers, and the invocation of spiritual guidance, all of which are essential elements in a fighter's preparation for combat.

Krabi-Krabong:
The Thai Art of Sword and Staff

Krabi-Krabong is another traditional Thai martial art that combines weaponry with the unarmed combat techniques of Muay Boran, rooted in ancient warfare when these skills were essential on the battlefield. The name refers to the primary weapons used in the art: the *krabi* (sword) and *krabong* (staff). However, the system includes a variety of other weapons, such as spears, clubs, shields, and double swords, making it a comprehensive martial art for both armed and unarmed combat.

Kings, soldiers, and warriors alike have practiced Krabi-Krabong throughout Thai history, and it has become a cornerstone of Thai cultural identity. In ancient Siam, Krabi-Krabong was practiced not only by soldiers but also by warrior monks, who combined their martial training with deep spiritual practices. Krabi-Krabong is even believed to have originated at Buddhai Swan (Wat Phutthaisawan) in Ayutthaya, a temple founded by King Ramathibodi (Pra-chao Uthong), the first king of Ayutthaya, in 1350. Many legendary figures, including King Naresuan, Prince Ekathotsarot, King Taksin, and Pra Patt'a Yodt Fa Chulalok, are reputed to have studied at this temple. The system taught at Buddhai Swan is believed to be that of Major General Pra Arjarn Prong and Pichai Sung Kran, two significant figures in the development of Krabi-Krabong.

The Buddhai Swan Temple played a crucial role in shaping Thailand's martial history, and it is often said that Thailand's very existence owes much to the training and discipline imparted at this place of learning. Although Buddhism values nonviolence and compassion, this was balanced with the practical need for self-defense. These practitioners were often trained to protect their temples and communities, embodying the concept of righteous warfare where combat was not driven by aggression but by the necessity to defend the kingdom, temple, and people.

Temples in ancient Siam served as more than just spiritual centers; they were also places of learning for various disciplines, including martial arts. Monks, alongside teaching spiritual wisdom, often instructed students in physical skills to safeguard the surrounding community during times of unrest. An example of this is the revered Buddhist monk Phor Than Mar, who founded the Muay Boran style of Muay Chaiya style, demonstrating how monks were integral to both spiritual and martial education.

At Wat Phutthaisawan, the blending of spiritual and martial disciplines was a real and essential part of Thai history. Buddhist monks at the temple taught swordsmanship and instilled in warriors the moral principles necessary to become righteous defenders of the kingdom. Warriors trained in Krabi-Krabong at Wat Phutthaisawan were not only skilled in combat but also bound by Buddhist values, which included:

- Always speak the truth.
- Never take a life unjustly.
- Refrain from stealing.
- Avoid alcohol.
- Abstain from reprehensible sexual conduct.

These principles ensured that the warriors were not only effective on the battlefield but also morally upright, reflecting the Buddhist ethos of righteous warfare and compassionate conduct.

As in Muay Boran, Krabi-Krabong practitioners performed the Wai Khru ceremony during training sessions and before battle, paying respect to their teachers, ancestors, and the sacred lineage of their art form. Their weapons were often blessed by monks to imbue them with spiritual protection, reflecting the belief that every aspect of martial arts from the crafting of weapons to the execution of techniques carries profound spiritual significance.

Mindfulness was a central concept in Krabi-Krabong training, as warriors were taught to maintain full awareness in the present moment as a single distraction in battle could mean death. This heightened sense of focus allowed them to read their opponent's movements and respond with precision, ensuring that their reactions were swift, calculated, and effective.

This mental discipline was cultivated through intense training and real-life battle experiences. Yet this mindfulness transcended combat, helping warriors develop mental clarity and emotional balance in their everyday lives. Through disciplined training and meditation, practitioners also learned to harness their life force energy or *Lom* (wind energy), believed to circulate through the body. By mastering this energy, they enhanced both their physical capabilities and their spiritual connection, reinforcing the idea that mastery of the body and mind together could lead to spiritual enlightenment.

Krabi-Krabong warriors trained to know their weapons as an extension of their body and soul. The movements of the krabi and krabong would be practiced until they became fluid and intuitive, embodying the inner calm of the warrior. The seamless interaction between body, weapon, and spirit exemplifies the philosophy that mastery over the self is key to mastering any external force.

This Siamese martial art was forged through the realities of war, evolving and refining itself over centuries. It is said that Krabi-Krabong incorporated elements from neighboring martial traditions, making it a highly adaptable and versatile system. Its techniques are believed to include influences from Indian Silambam, Indonesian sword fighting, Burmese Banshay, and Cambodian Kbach Kun Boran. By absorbing the finest techniques from these systems, Krabi-Krabong became one of the most effective sword-fighting styles of its time, playing a crucial role in defending the Siamese people and their kingdom from external threats.

The highly effective weapon and hand-to-hand combat system of Krabi-Krabong has long been the martial art taught to the entire Thai Army, and its influence continues to this day. Although firearms and modern tactics now dominate warfare, Krabi-Krabong is still an integral part of training for the Thai military and police, ensuring that this ancient tradition continues to shape Thailand's defense forces.

Sport duels in Krabi-Krabong still exist, though they are far less common than other Thai martial arts. Wat Phutthaisawan is one of the few places reported to continue teaching this traditional weapon system, and a handful of institutes in Thailand,

Europe, the United Kingdom, and the United States also offer training in Krabi-Krabong. The art is also showcased at the World Martial Arts Council Games in Bangkok, where athletes compete in protected bouts using foam weapons to ensure safety while preserving the spirit of the martial art.

More than just a sword-fighting system, Krabi-Krabong combines martial prowess with spiritual guidance, making it a sacred art of life and death. Deeply interwoven with Thailand's spiritual and cultural history, Krabi-Krabong's legacy endures as a vital link between the past and present in Thailand's martial traditions.

CHAPTER SIX

FROM ANCIENT WARFARE TO THE SPORT OF MUAY THAI

AWAKENING WARRIOR SPIRIT

In my early twenties, I became fully committed to self-healing and living a disciplined, warrior-monk-like path of martial training and personal growth, yet I sometimes found myself distracted and drawn into romantic relationships, nudging me to embrace life's lighter moments.

During this time, I also developed a passion for filmmaking. My martial training at that time ran parallel to an apprenticeship at Lone Woolfe Productions, where I learned filmmaking from my mentors Mike and Niki Woolfe, a couple passionate about creative arts. This pursuit expanded my knowledge of global mythology, African history, and untold stories from cultures around the world. My first project took me to Sierra Leone, where I directed *The Lion Mountains: A Journey Through Sierra Leone's History*. This was my first visit to Africa and the first time anyone in my African Caribbean family had returned to the continent since the transatlantic slave trade had carried them away. It was a deeply personal journey, as I confronted the painful legacy of slavery and British colonialism, but ultimately it reconnected me with my African roots, broadened my global perspective, and deepened my storytelling skills.

As I sought more opportunities for growth in Muay Thai, I discovered KO Combat Academy, a highly competitive Muay Thai club in East and North London. This was a turning point in my martial arts journey.

KO Combat Academy was founded in 1976 by Bill Judd, an East Londoner of Irish descent known for his tough Muay Thai training and for producing champion fighters. The North London branch where I trained was led by Arjan Vinny Deckon, a commanding instructor of Nigerian and Irish heritage born in Liverpool. His teaching style was rooted in traditional Thai techniques, combined with a strict, no-nonsense approach focused on strength, fitness, and hard sparring. The training atmosphere felt like a military camp, ideal for serious students.

From the start, I felt out of my depth, but still I thrived on the challenge. The training was intense, starting with several rounds of skipping rope or shadowboxing, followed by a mix of push-ups, squats, dips, and sit-ups. But that was only the warm-up. After stretching, we worked on fight techniques, pad drills, and a minimum of fifteen rounds of sparring. Under Arjan Vinny's mentorship, I quickly refined my skills, focusing on defensive techniques due to my ongoing injuries. I shifted away from heavy kicks, instead honing my punches, low kicks, and knee strikes.

Training with Arjan V also introduced me to Muay Boran, teaching me techniques not only for inside the ring, like Muay Thai, but also for the battlefield—a discipline designed for war. Muay Boran training was grueling, with intense conditioning exercises before learning forms and combat techniques. We practiced sequences involving locks, breaks, takedowns, killing moves, and strategic strikes for attacks and defense. These sessions fully woke up my warrior spirit and toughened me up both mentally and physically.

We explored the cultural and historical significance of each move, learning their names in Thai. I delved further into Krabi-Krabong, a weapons system using double swords or a shield and sword. Arjan V also introduced me to a grading system developed by the Kru Muay Thai Association and Grand Masters in Thailand, which provided a structured approach to learning both Muay Thai and Muay Boran. This set me apart as a fighter with a unique blend of ancient and modern skills—something few gyms in the UK offered. Many focused solely on the sports aspect of Muay Thai, while overlooking the cultural heritage.

Through both martial arts and filmmaking, I followed a path of self-discovery and personal growth. These practices became the cornerstones of my life, offering me the discipline, focus, and strength to explore new avenues and gain valuable life experiences. They provided a foundation for my personal development and shaped the way I engage with the world.

The Evolution of Muay Boran into Muay Thai

As I've already described, the ancient Siamese practiced Muay Boran primarily for self-defense and combat. Its techniques were initially crafted to equip warriors for battle, with the skills learned essential for survival in warfare, particularly when close fighting was prevalent and warriors might lose their weapons. This highly effective fighting system with all its variations enabled warriors to utilize their own bodies as weapons during intense combat situations.

However, over time, Muay Boran evolved beyond its military roots. It became part of local cultural heritage, and demonstrations took place during festivals and celebrations. This gradually led to more organized competitive tournaments as a way to showcase skill, bravery, and physical prowess in front of the community and for royalty.

These ancient tournaments were intense, often brutal events distinct from modern Muay Thai competitions although they were significant demonstrations of skill, bravery, and resilience. Fighters competed without gloves, wrapping their hands in cotton or hemp ropes (*Kard Chuek*), which provided only minimal protection but intensified the force and damage from each strike.

Each fighter represented a unique regional Muay Boran style— Muay Chaiya, Muay Korat, Muay Lopburi, Muay Tha Sao, and many others. These variations allowed fighters to broadcast their unique heritage incorporating powerful elbow and knee strikes, grappling, and clinching techniques while testing both physical prowess and mental toughness against other disciplines.

Tournaments were popular attractions during festivals, religious celebrations, and royal events, drawing large audiences and creating a festive atmosphere. Often held under royal patronage, these challenges provided kings a chance to scout skilled warriors for their armies. Victorious fighters earned rewards, titles, and sometimes positions in the royal guard, elevating their social status.

With minimal safety measures and no standardized rules, these matches were highly dangerous, often continuing until one fighter could no longer stand due to exhaustion, injury, or being knocked out. There were no time limits or scoring systems. Emphasis was placed on endurance, strength, and technical skill—qualities that remain integral to Muay Thai today.

In the early twentieth century, Siam experienced major changes as it aimed to modernize its politics, society, and culture. The transformation of Muay Boran into the modern sport of

Muay Thai was significantly influenced by the heightened exposure to Western sports and culture as part of a larger international engagement driven by colonial threats and the pressures of international relations. At the same time the demand for battlefield fighting techniques decreased significantly as the nation evolved into a more peaceful society.

The Siamese military was instrumental in the pivotal shift of Muay Boran into a developed sport. It utilized Muay Boran not only to train soldiers but also to preserve and elevate the martial arts. The regional styles of Muay Boran each contributed unique elements that laid the foundation for modern Muay Thai as a national sport. These ancient systems, once purely focused on lethal and disabling techniques, evolved to emphasize knockout power, defensive strategies, technical striking, and agility as the more deadly moves were removed for competitive events. The combined knowledge from these styles became the basis for a versatile and dynamic combat sport, balancing offense and defense, strength and finesse. This blend of regional expertise ensures that the essence of Thailand's ancient martial arts lives on in contemporary Muay Thai, preserving its heritage while adapting to modern competition.

A key aspect of this modernization effort was the adoption of Western-style boxing gloves, replacing the traditional Kard Chuek to enhance safety and align with international boxing standards. There was also the establishment of standardized rules, the introduction of referees, the implementation of time-limited rounds, and relocating fights from open spaces to a Western-style boxing ring.

On June 23, 1939, Siam also officially changed its name to Thailand. This shift was part of a broader nationalistic effort led by Prime Minister Field Marshal Plaek Phibunsongkhram to fortify the country's independence during a time of regional colonial threats. The new name, meaning "land of the free," emphasizes the nation's historical independence and highlights a distinct identity meant to unify the country's diverse ethnic groups and strengthen the sense of a cohesive state.

The military played its own a key role by formalizing Muay Thai, helping it evolve into a regulated sport with standardized practices. As part of this transition, many of the lethal Muay Boran techniques were banned or rendered impractical due to the introduction of new rules. This shift led to a decline in the widespread practice of Muay Boran, confining it to specific groups and paving the way for the rise of modern Muay Thai.

The creation of formal sports venues like Rajadamnern Stadium in 1945 provided a structured environment for regular Muay Thai competitions. In 1956, the establishment of Lumpinee Boxing Stadium further solidified Muay Thai's place in Thai culture, and it became one of the most iconic venues for the sport. Lumpinee played a crucial role in showcasing the evolution of Muay Thai as it shifted from its ancient Muay Boran roots to the highly competitive modern version. Fighters who competed at Lumpinee were regarded as the best in the world, and the stadium became a symbol of Thailand's rich martial arts tradition.

As Muay Thai evolved into a national sport and cultural emblem, it also gained international fame. However, this transition from a traditional martial art to a competitive sport shifted focus from deeper martial values to athletic prowess and victory in the ring. This change aligned with broader societal shifts but moved away from the deeper spiritual and self-mastery aspects historically integral to its practice.

The commercialization of Muay Thai brought significant global recognition but also introduced challenges. The gambling industry became even more influential, intertwining financial interests with the sport's outcomes often at the expense of martial ethics. This aspect of modern competition has led to the exploitation of fighters, especially young athletes from disadvantaged backgrounds, prioritizing immediate financial gains over their long-term health and development.

Today, while Muay Thai is celebrated worldwide for its effectiveness and dynamic moves, there's growing concern about preserving its rich underpinnings and ensuring ethical practices. This includes addressing the impacts of commercialization and gambling, protecting young fighters, and maintaining the sport's integrity and traditional values.

When comparing traditional martial arts with combative ring sports, we can notice that traditional arts typically emphasize introspection, self-awareness, integrity, and personal development. They guide students to view self-protection as a means to achieve higher goals and a more fulfilling inner life. On the other hand, combat sports and fighting tournaments typically emphasize external validation while measuring success more strictly based on wins and losses. This approach can encourage an ego-driven mindset, where the pursuit of public affirmation and competitive success overshadows the deeper values.

In the modern world, fighters are challenged to integrate both internal growth and external achievement. Competitions become opportunities to test oneself and not just to win but to evolve as a practitioner and individual. This path demands a balanced use of the ego, employing it as a tool without allowing it to dominate. It involves leveraging all experiences, good and bad, for greater understanding. By unifying the internal virtues of traditional martial arts with the external challenges of competition, one can embody the spirit of a noble warrior, making each moment a step toward greater personal and communal development.

Thai martial arts offer this path as they are deeply interwoven with spiritual traditions, rituals, and a cultural heritage that empower not only the fighters but also their teachers and more introspective practitioners. These practices go beyond physical training, embedding values of respect, humility, and discipline into each step of a martial artist's journey. These spiritual dimensions transform Thai martial arts from mere combat techniques into a holistic system that honors tradition, strengthens character, and celebrates the resilience of the Thai people.

MUAY THAI ON THE WORLD STAGE

Muay Thai has steadily risen from a traditional combat art in Thailand to a globally recognized sport, largely due to its effectiveness and the dedication of fighters and promoters. Throughout the twentieth century, Thai fighters began participating in international martial arts competitions, impressing audiences worldwide with their endurance, technique, and devastating power. As these fighters consistently defeated opponents from other disciplines, Muay Thai's reputation as a lethal and efficient fighting system spread around the globe.

During World War I, Thai soldiers stationed in France seized the opportunity to showcase Muay Thai as part of a cultural exchange to boost morale. Skilled fighters organized matches where French boxers competed against them. This was one of the first occasions when foreigners were introduced to Muay Thai outside Thailand. These exchanges were more than mere exhibitions, as they allowed the Thai military to demonstrate their national identity through martial prowess.

The 1980s and early 1990s are widely regarded as the golden era of Muay Thai, marked by the emergence of legendary fighters who elevated the sport to global prominence. Samart Payakaroon, widely regarded as one of the greatest Muay Thai fighters of all time, also won the WBC Junior Welterweight boxing title in 1986. Like many Thai fighters, Samart was ambidextrous and often switched stances during his fights. His signature technique was the teep (front push kick), which he used like a jab in boxing to measure distance and control his opponent. Samart's push kick was so powerful that he was known to knock out opponents with it—a feat in Muay Thai. It's believed that he developed this technique to protect his face from cuts and scars, as he was considered quite handsome and wanted to avoid damage during fights.

During this time, foreign fighters also began to make their mark. One of the most influential was Ramon "The Diamond" Dekkers from the Netherlands, widely considered one of the most well-known foreign Muay Thai fighters. Dekkers made his Thai debut in 1990, fighting Namphon Nongkeepayayuth at Lumpinee Stadium, and went on to face many other top Thai fighters. His victories over Thai fighters helped him gain recognition as one of the first non-Thais to successfully compete at the highest levels of Muay Thai.

Another notable foreigner was Dany Bill, a Cameroonian fighter who grew up in France. A contemporary of Dekkers, Bill was renowned for his technical skill, especially his sweeping techniques and precision. He became one of the most respected foreign Nak Muays of the 1990s, taking on the best Thai fighters and mastering the traditional Muay Thai style.

The tourism boom in Thailand in the 1980s and 1990s helped spread Muay Thai. Martial arts enthusiasts and travelers flocked to Thailand to experience the sport firsthand. This influx of international interest led to the establishment of Muay Thai gyms around the world, especially in the United States, the UK, the Netherlands, Europe, and Australia. As Muay Thai gained a following, it became an important element of the global martial arts scene.

The 1990s and 2000s saw mixed martial arts (MMA) rise in popularity, providing a new platform for Muay Thai. MMA fighters seeking to improve their striking techniques quickly adopted

Muay Thai for its devastating elbows, knees, and clinch control. The sport's effectiveness in close-range combat earned it global recognition. Fighters like Randy Couture, Georges St-Pierre, and Anderson Silva integrated Muay Thai into their training, cementing it as a critical component of modern MMA.

The early 2000s saw the release of one of the most exciting martial arts films: *Ong-Bak* starring Tony Jaa. It introduced the dynamic fighting style of Muay Boran to a worldwide audience, highlighting its distinctive techniques and cultural importance. These developments helped establish Muay Thai as more than just a sport, but a symbol of Thai national pride and martial discipline.

Today, Muay Thai is practiced in nearly every corner of the world, with thousands of gyms dedicated to teaching it. The sport has become a staple in kickboxing, MMA, and even fitness circles. The rigorous training involved in Muay Thai, which emphasizes strength, endurance, flexibility, and discipline, has made it a favorite of fitness enthusiasts and professional fighters alike.

Muay Thai's rise from a battlefield art in ancient Thailand to a globally recognized sport is a testament to its enduring effectiveness and adaptability. Muay Thai's cultural traditions, including the Wai Khru (traditional prefight ritual) and the Ram Muay (war dance), are respected by fighters globally. These traditions help to preserve Muay Thai's spiritual and philosophical legacy while making it accessible to a new generation of practitioners worldwide.

Muay Thai's influence has even spread to military and police training worldwide, recognized for its practicality and efficiency in self-defense situations.

Major international competitions, such as ONE Championship, Glory Kickboxing, and the World Muay Thai Championships, showcase top-tier Thai fighters alongside international challengers, further promoting the sport on a global scale. Thai fighters continue to be revered as the gold standard in Muay Thai, but today, athletes from countries like the United Kingdom, France, the United States, Australia, and the Netherlands compete at the highest levels, blending Muay Thai with other martial arts to create dynamic and innovative fighting styles.

Muay Thai, with its ancient origins blending physical effectiveness and spiritual depth, has become a unique and influential force in the martial arts world. Its rich cultural traditions continue to inspire practitioners around the globe, ensuring that the legacy of this time-honored art will endure for generations to come.

The Spiritual Traditions within Thai Martial Arts

Thai spirituality plays a profound role in the development and practice of Krabi-Krabong, Muay Boran, and Muay Thai. It is woven into every aspect, shaping not only how fighters approach combat but also the rituals and values that guide their training and discipline. These martial arts draw from Buddhist principles of mindfulness and moral conduct, animistic beliefs in protective spirits, and Hindu myths of channeling the power of gods and natural forces.

Esoteric knowledge and magical rituals, such as the use of mantras, spells, prayers, and chants, are believed to summon protective spirits, enhance mental clarity, and fortify the fighter's spirit during battle. These practices sharpen the warrior's focus and connect them to deeper spiritual forces, reflecting the profound blend of martial skill and mysticism that has long defined Thailand's rich traditions.

Though Muay Boran and Krabi-Krabong warriors were known for their physical dominance and deadly fighting abilities, their practices are deeply rooted in Buddhist principles of humility, respect, moral conduct, and right action.

Key techniques, such as maintaining a grounded posture, balance, effective defense, pushing through challenges, and developing a heightened awareness to read opponents, closely align with Buddhist teachings on mindfulness and the practice of detachment. Just as Buddhist monks strive to achieve mental distance from emotions and distractions, Thai warriors are trained to let go of fear, anger, and ego during both intense training and battle. They remain calm and present, focusing solely on the task at hand, rather than being swayed by the highs and lows of an engagement. In the heat of battle, fighters must stay centered and free from emotions to respond with clarity rather than impulse. This mental discipline is one of the deeper values that guide Muay Boran, Krabi-Krabong, and Muay Thai, elevating them beyond physical combat to a path of inner strength and self-mastery.

It was common for Muay Boran fighters to seek Buddhist protection and blessings from a monk before a conflict, with the goal to invoke spiritual guidance and mental clarity. The prefight rituals of Wai Khru and Ram Muay engage mindful movements to both ready a warrior for battle and to connect them to their lineage. They emphasize the belief in spiritual protection and guidance. In harmony with their Wai Khru and Ram Muay, warriors often recite Buddhist vows such as: "I Take Refuge in the Buddha! I Take Refuge in the Dhamma! I Take Refuge in the Sangha! I Take Refuge in the Triple Gem!"

Animistic beliefs in spiritual entities inhabiting natural objects play a critical role in Thai martial arts as well. Many warriors wear sacred amulets and are anointed with sacred tattoos to give them protection from guardian spirits. These amulets and tattoos are often provided by special monks or teachers and infused with spiritual energy for safeguarding them and bringing good luck in battle.

Thai spiritual mythology, particularly the Ramakien, influences the choice of imagery in these talismans, making symbolic connections to the gods, nature, and ancestral spirits. Fighters are thought to channel the powers of deities like Hanuman, the monkey god, and Pha Ram, the incarnation of the Hindu protector god Vishnu, invoking qualities such as speed, agility, strength, and accuracy during combat. Hanuman's wind-like agility and unpredictable movements are particularly embodied in styles emphasizing swift footwork, jumping attacks, and evasive techniques.

As taught to me by Grand Master Woody of the Kru Muay Thai Association in Bangkok, a warrior's connection to the natural elements of wind, earth, fire, water and metal represents traits essential in battle: Wind symbolizes speed and evasion, allowing the fighter to move fluidly and unpredictably. Earth signifies grounding and resilience, reflecting stability and strength in the face of adversity. Fire embodies transformation and passion, fueling the fighter's determination and intensity. Water represents adaptability and fluidity, teaching the warrior to flow with the fight and react to changing circumstances. Lastly, metal represents hardness and discipline, empowering an unwavering willpower and unbreakable resolve. These elements are more than metaphors; they reflect a deeply spiritual belief that fighters harmonize their actions with the forces of nature, creating a balance between their physical abilities and the natural world around them. This connection between the elements and combat is part of the spiritual essence that defines Thai martial arts, where mastery of oneself and the environment is as important as technical skill.

Thai warriors honor their ancestors and often call upon the spirits of past warriors for strength and guidance. This practice enhances their connection to their heritage, empowering them mentally, physically, and spiritually. In the chapters that follow, we will look in more detail at the ways Muay Thai is intertwined with Thai spiritual traditions and cultural heritage.

CHAPTER SEVEN

SACRED MUAY THAI RITUALS AND PRACTICES

HUMBLENESS, RESPECT, AND DEDICATION

As I immersed myself in the rigorous training regimen of a professional fighter, I discovered that the skills and principles I was learning were not confined to the gym. They empowered every facet of my life, guiding me down a unique path shaped by the warrior's code of humbleness, respect, and dedication. These principles passed down to me by Arjan Vinny, who in turn had received them from Grand Master Woody and Grand Master Phosawat of Thailand, hold profound significance in the realms of both martial arts and Buddhism. *Humbleness* deepened my interconnectedness with all living beings and nurtured a sense of self-awareness and empathy within me. *Respect* broadened my understanding that every being and every moment hold significance and emphasized the worth of all interactions. *Dedication* showed me the way to embody a wholehearted commitment to the path of a noble warrior, the guiding principles, and the relentless pursuit of excellence.

For many years my Sundays were devoted to intense martial arts training under Arjan V's guidance in Tottenham. These sessions not only brought us to peak physical fitness for combat but also fostered a sense of discipline, tested our personal limits, and became a spiritual journey for those seeking to go deeper. We often did weekly meditations at the beginning of the class, contemplating different topics such as giving and taking, respect and humility, impermanence, gratitude, equanimity, death, stillness, and more. The Sunday sessions were split into two consecutive classes that merged into one another, spanning from early afternoon to early evening. They catered to all levels, starting with general training and culminating in advanced sparring for professional fighters. This structure often transformed the day for some into a continuous four- to five-hour-long training marathon.

The sessions began with a rigorous two-hour regimen led by Arjan V, involving multiple rounds of intense rope-skipping, interspersed with demanding exercises like push-ups, squats, burpees, and sit-ups, ranging from twenty to fifty repetitions each. The experienced fighters set a relentless pace, challenging each participant to keep up or find a less intense spot on the fringes of the training floor. I thrived in the thick of it, pushing myself to the limits of my endurance. The philosophy was simple: "Train hard, and the battles will become easier."

During intense sessions, I often felt like I was pushing my strength and fitness to the brink, with my heart pounding so hard it seemed like it might explode, yet I found deep relief when I remembered to breathe more deeply. In hard sparring, it was always a choice: fight with all your might or take a beating and give up. Many times, even when I was losing, I discovered new depths of strength by refusing to quit, and fighting on until the end of the round, I often turned the round in my favor, revealing just how powerful my resolve could be when I refused to give up.

Transitioning from a fighter to a coach was a gradual process.

As I progressed through my grading, I began assisting with a Muay Thai class near London's Liverpool Street with my friend Fast Hands Shaz from All Stars. This was a class comprised of people seeking fitness and self-defense skills, and when Shaz relocated to Dubai, I took over teaching it. At the same time, Arjan V and a group of coaches, including myself, branched out to establish Muay Thai Masters Academy. My class in Liverpool Street became our first East London branch, and over the years, it experienced significant growth. There were just three regular students when I took over, but it evolved into a thriving class of thirty to forty students per session. I also assisted students in preparing for fights in both the UK and Thailand, leading them to personal and professional success.

Over the years, I've had the privilege of teaching thousands of students. I take great pride in guiding them as they develop new skills, conquer fears, improve their alignment, unlock their inner strength, and push their limits. Watching their growth in confidence and martial arts proficiency has been deeply rewarding and has brought me immense satisfaction.

MORE THAN JUST COMBAT:
CEREMONIES AND TRADITION

While Muay Thai is celebrated globally as a formidable combat sport, its roots reveal a complex intermixing of spiritual and cultural traditions that add depth and meaning to the physical practice. Integral ceremonies such as the Yok Kru and Krob Kru introduce students to the spiritual commitments and respect required in Muay Thai. These acceptance and initiation rituals forge a strong bond between teacher and student, establishing the ethos of humility, discipline, and dedication to one's teacher and the lineage. The Wai Khru ceremony and Ram Muay (war dance) are further expressions of this reverence, as fighters respectfully prepare the ring and offer homage to their teachers, ancestors, and spiritual protectors. These ceremonies harmoniously blend Buddhist, animistic, and Hindu traditions.

Another integral element is the traditional music of Sarama, a hauntingly beautiful and rhythmic accompaniment played live during the Wai Khru, Ram Muay, and fighting matches. Sarama music, performed with traditional instruments like the pi (Thai oboe), drums, and cymbals, sets the ceremonial tone, guiding fighters in their movements and serving as a spiritual backdrop to their ritual. This music heightens the atmosphere, connecting fighters and spectators to the historical and spiritual lineage of Muay Thai.

Even the unique ceremonial clothing and equipment worn in Muay Thai carry both practical and spiritual significance. Items like the Mongkon (headpiece) and Pra Jiads (armbands) symbolize protection, tradition, and respect for the art. The ceremonial way they are put on before a fight reminds the warrior of the psychological resilience and mental fortitude developed in Muay Thai training. Fighters learn to move beyond fear, pain, and aggression, focusing on precision and strategy.

Exploring these spiritual dimensions in greater detail, beginning with the Yok Kru and Krob Kru initiation rituals, the significance of ceremonial clothing, and culminating with the Wai Khru and Ram Muay, reveals the intricate interplay between Muay Thai's physical demands and its spiritual foundations.

Yok Kru Ceremony: Accepting a Student

The Yok Kru, or acceptance ceremony, in Muay Thai and other Thai martial arts, marks the formal initiation of a student under a teacher's guidance and establishes a profound bond of respect and dedication. Historically, students underwent a trial period under the teacher's watchful eye to demonstrate commitment before being officially accepted into the training camp. Once that trial period was over, students would partake in the Yok Kru ceremony, typically conducted on Thursdays—a day deemed auspicious in Thai culture.

The ceremony involves offering three white lotus blossoms or jasmine garlands, a white candle, and training fees, symbolizing respect, purity of intention, and dedication to learning. Through this ritual, the student publicly acknowledges the teacher's role as a mentor and commits fully to the discipline and philosophy of the art. The Yok Kru ceremony blends Buddhist, Brahmin, and animistic traditions, using offerings, blessings, and the auspicious timing to establish a sacred bond between teacher and student.

In modern practices, where training timelines are often shorter, an interview can sometimes replace the traditional trial period. However, the Yok Kru ceremony remains a powerful symbol of a student's readiness and willingness to uphold the teacher's guidance and embody the values of the martial art.

Krob Kru Ceremony: Completing the Teacher

The Krob Kru ceremony is a Thai ritual in disciplines like martial arts, classical dance, and traditional arts where students formally honor and accept their teacher's guidance. Translating to "completing the teacher," Krob Kru symbolizes the student's recognition of the teacher's role in imparting not only technical skills but also moral and ethical wisdom. Rooted in Hindu-Brahmin beliefs blended with Thai Buddhist traditions, the ceremony reflects deep respect, gratitude, and dedication to one's mentor.

During the Krob Kru, the teacher's headpiece is placed over the student's, signifying their acceptance as a disciple and invoking the teacher's grace and protection for the student's success and growth. The ceremony includes offerings and prayers to honor teachers, instill commitment in students, seek forgiveness for past errors, and reinforce mindful living under the teacher's guidance.

In Thai, the term *Kru* means teacher. In Thai culture, there are different types of teachers who are held in high regard for educating students. And teachers can come in various forms:

- Divine figures: deities such as Buddha, Vishnu, Shiva, and others
- Ruesi sages: revered esoteric hermit sages with diverse spiritual practices
- Human teachers: instructors both within formal education and traditional arts

Each type holds unique virtues and is believed to guide, support, and bless students on their path toward success.

MUAY THAI KRU: GUIDING THE WAY

The role of a Kru, or teacher, in Muay Thai extends well beyond instruction in fighting techniques. A Muay Thai Kru embodies mentorship, moral guidance, and spiritual leadership, making them a figure of profound respect and dedication within the

Thai martial arts community. The teacher-student relationship is a lifelong bond, rooted in loyalty and gratitude.

A Kru serves not only as a coach but also a moral compass, instilling values like discipline, humility, and respect. These values align closely with Buddhist principles of detachment from ego and resilience, positioning Muay Thai as both a physical journey in martial mastery and a path of personal growth.

Beyond physical training, the Kru provides spiritual protection and blessings. Once this sacred bond is established in the Yok Kru ceremony, the Kru serves as a guardian and conveyor of ancient Muay Thai techniques, rituals, and cultural practices. With ceremonies like the Wai Kru and Ram Muay, which enrich the fighter's spirit and honor and tradition, the Kru connects students to the deeper cultural and spiritual heritage of Muay Thai.

A Kru in Muay Thai possesses extensive knowledge that extends beyond combat skills to include traditional healing, nutrition, physical conditioning, and sacred ceremonies. Through their teaching, a Kru shapes not only skilled fighters but also respectful individuals who embody the spirit of a true warrior. The path of a Kru is therefore one of sacred duty and profound influence within Thai martial arts.

Building on the foundation set by a Kru, an *Arjan*, meaning "master," represents a teacher who has achieved deep expertise, respect, and knowledge in Muay Thai. An Arjan is not only highly skilled in the techniques of Muay Thai but also deeply knowledgeable of its cultural, historical, and spiritual aspects. They serve as mentors to other Krus, coaches, and students, passing down traditional practices, rituals, and moral guidance.

At the pinnacle of Muay Thai is the title of *Bravarjan*, meaning "grand master," reserved for those who have dedicated their lives to preserving and advancing Muay Thai. A Bravarjan is seen as a guardian of the art's heritage. They embody Muay Thai's deepest values and traditions, mastering technical skills as well as the spiritual, cultural, and historical foundations of the art.

Ceremonial Clothing in Muay Thai

Within Muay Thai traditions each item of a Nak Muay's attire and equipment carries significance. Each piece not only serves a practical function but also symbolically reflects beliefs in spiritual protection, respect for teachers, and honoring tradition.

Mongkon (Headpiece)

The Mongkon is a sacred headpiece worn by Muay Thai fighters during the Wai Kru Ram Muay prefight ritual that expresses respect for teachers and tradition.

Traditionally, the Mongkon is crafted from a narrow strip of cloth twisted into a cord, and some versions are inscribed with sacred Sanskrit symbols or magical spells. These may include Buddhist mantras, like NA MO BUDDHAYA (invoking the protection of the Buddha), or yantras (sacred geometric patterns) that are believed to provide spiritual protection, enhance power, and ensure success in battle. The Mongkon is typically blessed by a monk or a Kru before being placed on the fighter's head, reinforcing it as a conduit for spiritual protection and good fortune, while also connecting the fighter to their lineage and tradition.

Beyond its spiritual power, the Mongkon serves as a tangible representation of the fighter's respect and devotion to their teacher, gym, and the art of Muay Thai. In some schools, the Mongkon color may indicate the fighter's experience or mastery, similar to a belt system in other martial arts. However, this is not universal. Also in some Muay Thai camps it is considered bad luck for the fighters to even handle the Mongkon themselves. Only the Kru or Arjan may touch it, ceremoniously placing it on the fighter's head before the Wai Kru ritual and removing it before the fight begins. This process highlights the connection between spiritual preparation and the physical act of combat, reinforcing the balance between the mental and physical aspects of Muay Thai.

In essence, the Mongkon is not merely a ceremonial decoration; it represents the fusion of spiritual belief, empowerment, protection, and a martial tradition that is the heart of Muay Thai. It serves as both a protector and a symbol of the discipline, respect, and spirituality that define a fighter's path as a warrior.

Pra Jiads (Armbands)

The Pra Jiads, cloth armbands worn around the biceps, are an essential part of a fighter's attire in Muay Thai. Much like the Mongkon, these armbands are far from mere accessories; they represent protection, good fortune, and the fighter's heritage.

The tradition of wearing Pra Jiads dates back to ancient times when Muay Boran warriors would tear pieces of cloth from their loved ones' clothing—often their mother's or another family member—before heading into battle. These handmade armbands connected the fighter and their home. The act of crafting or giving the Pra Jiad, whether by a family member or a teacher, enhances its meaning, embodying the blessings, protection, and support of those wishing the fighter success and safety. They serve as symbols of courage, honor, and loyalty, reflecting the fighter's bond with their family, gym, and martial traditions.

The presence of the Pra Jiads reminded warriors who they were fighting for, empowering them symbolically with a sense of love and protection. It was like carrying a piece of home onto the battlefield or into the ring, like a physical manifestation of emotional strength and familial support, believed to bring good luck and spiritual protection.

In some Muay Thai camps, Pra Jiads are colored to match the Mongkon, reflecting a fighter's rank or proficiency. However, this practice is not universal and varies according to the traditions of each training camp.

While some fighters choose to wear one Pra Jiad, others wear two. This can be a matter of personal preference or tradition, often seen as a way to ensure balance and protection for both sides of the body and the equal distribution of blessings and good fortune during combat.

Kard Chuek (Hand Wraps)

Kard Chuek refers to the traditional hand wraps used by Muay Boran warriors to protect their hands and damage their opponents. These wraps were typically made from hemp ropes or cotton cloth strips and were used to enclose the hands, knuckles, and wrists, extending sometimes from the fingers all the way to the elbow. Unlike the padded boxing gloves used today, Kard Chuek provided minimal cushioning, which heightened the intensity of strikes and added a brutal dimension to combat. The rough texture of hemp rope could inflict significant damage to opponents, particularly when hitting with the knuckles.

However, the use of Kard Chuek was not just practical but also ritualistic. Wrapping the hands was an important prefight tradition—a mindfulness practice that established a fighter's combat readiness and respect for their martial traditions. Some fighters would perform this ritual with added spiritual significance, incorporating prayers or blessings into the process. This ritualization reinforced the connection between physical combat and spiritual protection, with some fighters believing that these wraps, when blessed, could offer them not only physical fortitude but spiritual empowerment.

As Muay Boran transitioned into modern Muay Thai, the Kard Chuek gradually evolved into the more standardized hand wraps and boxing gloves used today. This change was part of an effort to increase safety measures and reduce the severity of injuries as modern rules and regulations were developed for Muay Thai competition. The introduction of padded gloves and cotton or elastic hand wraps helped protect fighters from the excessive damage associated with Kard Chuek while preserving the effectiveness of strikes.

Phakaoma (Loincloth)

The Phakaoma (also spelled Pha Khao Ma) is a traditional multipurpose cloth that has been used for centuries in various ways, including as a loincloth, garment, headscarf, towel, or bag. In the context of Muay Boran, the Phakaoma was often worn as a loincloth during training or combat.

Made from a single piece of fabric, this was skillfully wrapped around the waist and passed between the legs, providing excellent freedom of movement and flexibility—both essential for executing the dynamic techniques of Muay Boran. The Phakaoma was typically made from cotton or silk—materials that offered comfort and flexibility, crucial for the quick footwork, high kicks, knees, and evasive maneuvers central to Thai martial art.

While the Phakaoma didn't carry the same symbolic weight as the Mongkon or Pra Jiad, it still connected fighters to Thai cultural traditions and provided a simple, functional garment for training and battle.

As Muay Boran transitioned into modern Muay Thai, this loincloth was replaced by the Muay Thai shorts that are now standard attire in the sport. However, the Phakaoma is still worn in Muay Boran training and contests as well as during traditional ceremonies to honor the roots of Thai culture.

THE WAI KHRU:
PAYING RESPECT TO ONE'S TEACHERS

The Wai Khru ceremony is one of the most widely recognizable rituals in Muay Thai. The term *Wai* refers to the traditional Thai gesture of bowing with palms pressed together, while *Khru* or *Kru* means "teacher." Hence, *Wai Khru* translates to "Paying Respect to One's Teacher." This ritual is not exclusive to Muay Thai; it is also observed in Thai education, classical dance, and music to honor teachers and maintain a connection to tradition.

In Muay Thai, fighters perform this ritual to honor their teachers, ancestors, and the lineage of Muay Thai masters who have passed down the art through generations. It underscores the importance of respecting one's mentors and recognizing the value of their teachings. It is a link to the past, connecting the fighter to the long lineage of Muay Thai warriors, while also providing a moment of mental and spiritual focus. Through this ritual, combatants prepare for the fight by reflecting on their training, showing respect for their martial art, and mentally grounding themselves.

Historically, fighters would seek blessings from Buddhist monks or their Kru before entering combat. These blessings were meant to protect the fighter from harm and ensure good fortune. Sacred items like Mongkons (headbands) and Pra Jiads (armbands) were often blessed before a fight, imbuing them with spiritual power that connects the fighter to the divine. This belief in spiritual protection remains a direct connection to animist and Buddhist traditions in Thailand.

Before entering the ring, fighters bow three times in respect to their warrior traditions, often seen as an homage to the Three

Jewels of Buddhism: the Buddha, the Dharma, and the Sangha. Then once adorned with their Mongkon and Pra Jiads, the fighters enter the ring and move counterclockwise around it to spiritually seal it. As fighters circle the ring running their hand across the top rope, they closely inspect the fighting area, checking for any irregularities on the floor, ensuring the ropes are secure, and identifying potential distractions such as bright lights or key individuals in the crowd. This detailed examination of the environment allows fighters to familiarize themselves thoroughly with their surroundings—a crucial aspect of their strategic preparation. This symbolic act of sealing marks the ring as their territory, setting a mental and physical boundary for the contest ahead and mentally preparing them for the challenge.

As a fighter walks around the ring and bows in each corner, they invoke protection from their guiding spiritual forces. This aligns the fighter with principles of mindfulness, respect, and protection.

A fighter will eventually move to the center of the ring and gracefully transition from a standing position to kneeling on the floor. Typically, they face the direction of their gym or trainer, the judges, or sometimes a significant cultural or religious symbol in the arena, marking their respect for their tradition. The fighter brings their hands together in a prayerlike gesture, starting at the heart and then raising them to the forehead. This act is a sign of respect and humility. They then extend forward placing one hand on the floor, followed by the other, forming a triangle with their thumbs and first fingers. Bending forward, the fighter gently places their head between their hands on the ground in a deep bow. The fighter then bows one to three times symbolizing respect for their teachers, family, and godly forces. While some variations exist, with certain gyms assigning different meanings to the bows, the core practice of respect and mindfulness remains intact. As taught to me by Arjan Vinny in the UK and Grand Master Woody in Thailand, this three-bow tradition is deeply rooted in Muay Thai's spiritual and cultural legacy.

The Wai Khru is not just a physical ritual but a moment for meditation, prayer, and focus, allowing fighters to sharpen their mental clarity and ready themselves for the fight ahead. It serves as both a grounding tradition and a spiritual practice, reinforcing the deep respect at the core of Muay Thai.

The National Muay Thai Day celebrated on March 17 each year includes the Wai Khru Festival held at the ancient ruins of Ayutthaya. Students, fighters, and teachers from around the world gather to perform a collective Wai Khru, honoring the rich lineage of Muay Thai. The festival features cultural ceremonies, demonstrations, fighting tournaments, and blessings from Buddhist monks, underscoring the profound connection between Muay Thai and Thailand's spiritual and cultural heritage. The festival is more than a celebration of physical prowess; it is a tribute to the long-standing traditions and spiritual roots that make Muay Thai a unique martial art, steeped in cultural identity.

THE RAM MUAY: THE WAR DANCE

After completing the Wai Khru bows, the fighter proceeds with the Ram Muay, a personal and often gym-specific dance that highlights their readiness and pays homage to their lineage, region, or unique background. While the Wai Khru focuses on respect and gratitude, the Ram Muay is a personal display of the fighter's skill and identity. Often translated as the "Boxer's Dance" or the "War Dance," this is an essential prefight ritual integral to Muay Boran and Muay Thai tradition and another way for the fighter to ground themselves and connect spiritually and mentally to the task ahead. Each movement in the Ram Muay is meaningful, often reflecting the fighter's gym, lineage, and personal style while drawing on mythological, spiritual, and regional influences.

At its core, the Ram Muay is a way for fighters to display respect for their teachers and traditions. Each move in the dance can tell a story or embody key elements of Thai culture, such as Buddhism, animism, or mythological themes, like the Ramakien. The Ram Muay, like a moving meditation, serves as a way for fighters to clear their minds and focus their energy—just as the legendary Nai Khanomtom did before he fought and defeated the Burmese soldiers.

The Ram Muay has its origins in the ancient military traditions of Thai martial arts, developed during a time when Muay Boran was used in warfare. The War Dance was believed to invoke confidence and spiritual protection before battle, ensuring that warriors were fully prepared. As Muay Thai evolved from a battlefield art into a sport, the Ram Muay remained a key part of its ceremonial practice, preserving the rich history and traditions of Thailand.

After completing the respectful Wai Khru, the fighter, still adorned with their sacred Mongkon and Pra Jiads, begins to gracefully perform their dance. Each movement flows with intention and reverence, expressing their readiness and respect for the art of Muay Thai while drawing strength from the spiritual power imbued in their blessed attire. Over time, various styles of Ram Muay have emerged. Fighters from different regions incorporate distinct movements based on their local martial traditions. Some emphasize powerful, sweeping gestures to symbolize strength, while others highlight defensive stances that demonstrate resilience and strategic focus. Regional history, local beliefs, and the unique training of Muay Thai camps have influenced the attire, dance style, and expression seen during the Ram Muay.

Popular movements within the Ram Muay are often influenced by Thai mythology, especially tales from the Ramakien. One popular figure is Hanuman, the monkey god, who symbolizes agility, courage, and strength. Fighters frequently imitate Hanuman's

balance, leaping, and crouching movements to represent his loyalty and fearlessness. Similarly, Phra Ram, an incarnation of the
Hindu god Vishnu, inspires fighters to channel their precision
and strength. Fighters may mimic shooting arrows toward their
opponent, a symbolic act meant to intimidate and assert control,
mirroring Phra Ram's battle with Tosakan.

Another key spiritual element of the Ram Muay is the connection to nature, particularly Mother Earth. Fighters often
kneel, bow their heads, and swoop their hands across the ground,
symbolically drawing energy from the earth for protection and
stability. This act reflects animist beliefs, prevalent alongside
Buddhism in Thai culture. By channeling energy from the earth,
the fighter grounds themself physically, mentally, and spiritually,
embodying the resilience and stability of the earth.

Another spiritual influence in the Ram Muay linked to Hinduism and Buddhism is an acknowledgment of the Four Faces
of Phra Phrom representing the four cardinal directions of
north, east, south, and west. During the Ram Muay the fighter
consciously faces each direction while performing movements,
invoking spiritual protection from all sides. This act mirrors the
belief that Phra Phrom provides blessings and safeguards from
every direction, preparing the fighter for the match.

After completing the Ram Muay, the fighter's trainer removes
the Mongkon, signaling the end of the ritual. At this point, the
fighter is fully prepared—physically, mentally, and spiritually—for
the upcoming fight. It's much more than a warm-up; a fighter's
expression of their Ram Muay is often what first wins the crowd
and introduces them to the fighter's identity, personal strength,
grace, and skill while showcasing their readiness for battle.

The Ram Muay is a unique blend of athletic preparation, cultural expression, and spiritual practice, highlighting the deep
connection between Muay Thai and Thai cultural heritage.

TRADITIONAL MUSIC IN MUAY THAI: THE ROLE OF SARAMA

Alongside these Muay Thai traditions is the Sarama, the live rhythmic music that accompanies both the matches and the pre-fight rituals, creating a rich atmosphere and distinguishing Muay Thai from other forms of kickboxing. Performed by a Pi Muay ensemble, Sarama consists of three main instruments: the pi chawa (a quadruple-reed instrument with roots in India via Java), klong khaek drums (symbolizing male and female roles through syncopated rhythms called nathap), and ching cymbals (producing a beat known as ching chap). Together these instruments create a soundscape that is both hypnotic and energizing.

Originally, Sarama was performed in the Royal Court of Thailand, often alongside dramas featuring characters from Thai mythology. Today, Sarama can be enjoyed at cultural events, hotels, shopping malls, and most notably in Muay Thai stadiums, where it is often referred to as Phleng Pi Muay Thai.

Sarama is an improvisational piece of music led by the pi chawa player, performed at a slower, meditative pace during the Ram Muay to enhance the spiritual atmosphere as fighters pay respect and center themselves before the match. Then as the fight begins, the tempo of the Sarama quickens, mirroring the escalating energy and intensity of the fighters. This hypnotic rhythm provides psychological motivation and a guiding tempo, contrasting sharply with the fighters' swift, skillful, and often fierce movements. Serving as a live soundtrack, Sarama reflects and amplifies the fight's intensity, enriching the Muay Thai experience and creating a profound connection between fighters, audiences, and the sport's ancient traditions.

Muay Thai's traditions are deeply woven with practical, cultural, and spiritual significance, enriching both the practitioner and the art itself. From ceremonial clothing, such as the Mongkhon and Prajiad, which symbolize protection, good fortune, and connection to a fighter's heritage, to the intricate rituals and ceremonies, every element embodies respect, empowerment, history, and spiritual grounding. These traditions not only empower fighters but also provide a sense of greater purpose and mindfulness in their practice.

At the heart of Muay Thai training is the Muay Thai Kru (teacher), the mentor who imparts not only fighting techniques but also life lessons and martial values. Through rituals like the Wai Khru and Ram Muay, fighters express gratitude to their teachers, ancestors, and the art itself, forging a connection that transcends the physical.

Together these traditions unify Muay Thai as a holistic practice, blending physical prowess with cultural heritage and spiritual insight. They honor the roots of this ancient martial art while instilling enduring values that extend far beyond the ring.

CHAPTER EIGHT

ESOTERIC TRADITIONS WITHIN THAI MARTIAL ARTS

IN THE PURSUIT OF GLORY

From the beginning of my Muay Thai training, the prospect of competitive combat in the ring always appealed to me, but I hesitated to pursue it until I had addressed my physical limitations. As I cultivated a deeper respect for the warrior's code of humility, respect, and dedication, my interest in fighting for entertainment waned. Yet part of me still yearned to test my limits. Despite my limitations, my willpower drove me forward, and I held my own against professional fighters in our gym. The desire to challenge myself in the ring grew stronger, and my first opportunity came in the form of a twelve-man tournament called Ring Masters at the Excel Centre in East London.

At twenty-eight, I was a latecomer to ring fighting compared to the standards in Thailand, where children start fighting at six. The tournament required me to fight three times in a single day for a chance at victory. My first match was explosive. My opponent, a huge hulking figure, rushed me with a relentless barrage of punches. Arjan V's game plan had emphasized using kicks, as they scored higher, but I had to adapt quickly, relying on my hands and knees. Although the match was close, the judges gave the win to my opponent. That might have been the end of the tournament for me. However, when another fighter was disqualified, I got a second chance, and I jumped at the opportunity.

In the second fight, I took control right away, delivering strong punches, kicks, and knees that kept my opponent on the back foot. My footwork effectively maintained range, preventing him from closing in. I was winning the first two rounds when he landed a wild left hook, hitting me near the jaw and ear. The impact sent me tumbling to the canvas, dizzy and disoriented. Drawing on my training, I took an eight-count to regain my balance, using deep, steadying breaths to clear my head. By the time I stood back up, I was ready to fight again. My opponent tried to press his advantage, but I adopted a defensive stance, blocking his shots while countering with punches until the bell rang.

With Arjan V's words echoing in my mind, "You can do this, now go out there and finish him," I stepped into the third round with focus and determination. I unleashed a barrage of kicks followed by strong punches and knees, driving my opponent to the ropes, maintaining a solid defense, and delivering powerful counters. I relished every moment of the fight and delivered the win, advancing to the final round of the tournament.

My final opponent was Arnold Oborotov, a towering 6'5" fighter from KO Bloodline, a gym affiliated with ours run by Paul Marut, an ex-champion fighter from KO. Like Arjan V, Marut was known for producing strong, skilled Muay Thai fighters, and Oborotov was no exception. Despite my aching wrist and battered leg from the previous fights, I felt a surge of adrenaline. We exchanged respectful nods before launching into combat. I landed some solid punches, but Oborotov used his height and reach to his advantage, unleashing a barrage of leg kicks that targeted my right thigh. As

I pressed forward, Arjan V unexpectedly threw in the towel, concerned about the damage I had taken and wanting to prevent further injury. Though disappointed, I understood his decision. After the fight, Arjan honored me with the warrior name "LionHeart" in recognition of the determination and spirit I had shown. He acknowledged the moment I got back up after the eight-count in the second fight, noting that many would have given up, but I showed resilience and fought with the heart of a lion.

I left the tournament with a bruised ego and some physical injuries—a strained shoulder, wrist, and bruised leg—but it was a humbling and invaluable experience regarding fighting. I realized that injuries were an inherent part of the game, and given my physical limitations, I began to question pursuing a fighting career without first achieving physical balance and healing. Interestingly, Oborotov went on to become the British Muay Thai Kickboxing Champion and a two-time European Kickboxing Champion.

My own training evolved as I focused on finding physical balance, sharpening my abilities, and becoming a good coach. I channeled my energy into filmmaking and used my martial arts to enhance my practical fighting abilities and strengthen my fitness. As a dedicated coach, I became inspired to help others on their path to self-improvement, guiding them toward becoming the best versions of themselves and highly effective warriors.

THE POWER OF UNSEEN FORCES

One compelling aspect of Thai culture is its mystical traditions and esoteric practices, yet few foreigners really understand the spiritual elements that have shaped its practice throughout the centuries. Like many other aspects of Thai culture, these practices often blend Buddhist philosophy with animist beliefs, ancient ritualistic practices, and Hindu mythology and traditions. In essence, Muay Boran is much more than purely a method of self-defense, it is a spiritual discipline that embodies key values such as self-control, respect, honor, courage, and protection, both on the battlefield and in everyday life. Just as modern Muay Thai fighters perform the Wai Khru and Ram Muay before entering the ring to show respect and empower themselves both spiritually and physically, ancient Muay Boran warriors would invoke their warrior spirit and draw upon various esoteric traditions to enhance their strength and resilience during training and combat. Warriors showed a deep respect for their teachers, spiritual guardians, and the sacred knowledge that has been passed down through generations.

These esoteric practices take various forms such as magic spells, mantras and prayers, amulets and talismans, sacred tattoos, astrology and divination, rituals and ceremonies. These spiritual traditions are believed to enhance and protect a person's physical, psychological, and spiritual self.

Many ancient and modern warriors seek out certain monks and specialized practitioners to gain strength and spiritual protection. These figures, revered for their deep understanding of mystical practices, have played a crucial role in blending the physical and spiritual aspects of combat. Warriors would often receive magical amulets, charms, talismans, and magical tattoos and blessings from these sages to protect them and increase their skills and abilities for training and battle.

HERMITS OF MYSTICAL POWER:
THE RUESI MASTERS

In Thai folklore and literature, the Ruesi or Lersi are mystical hermit sages, revered figures deeply connected to ancient knowledge and esoteric wisdom. The term *Ruesi* originates from the Sanskrit word *rishi*, meaning "seer" or "sage." In the Vedic tradition, rishis are considered the sons of Brahma, credited with discovering or receiving many of the mantras found in the Vedas and other sacred texts. However, in everyday Thai conversations and modern cultural references, they are often referred to as Lersi rather than Ruesi. Both Lersi and Ruesi refer to the same figure, a hermit sage or seer who has mastered esoteric knowledge and spiritual practices.

In Thailand, the Ruesi trace their roots back to pre-Buddhist times during the Brahminist era, when they were believed to possess the ability to communicate with the gods and the supernatural realm. They were said to have mystical powers such as leaving their bodies, foreseeing the future, healing with forest plants, conversing with animals, and practicing early forms of alchemy. Over time, they became masters of herbal medicine, astrology, and magic and were seen as soothsayers or medicine men who lived in deep seclusion. The Ruesi typically resided in forests, spending their days in meditation and crafting potions to cure ailments, while enduring extreme physical and mental sacrifices to develop higher spiritual powers.

Their role in Thai culture extended beyond being mere healers or sages. The Ruesi are depicted as wise figures who guide kings, warriors, and common people, offering protection, blessings, and guidance. They are considered guardians of sacred knowledge, often retreating to temples or remote areas to meditate. In various rituals, Ruesi masks are worn to invoke their wisdom and spiritual protection, symbolizing a connection to powerful, ancient knowledge.

Across Southeast Asia the Ruesi are credited with compiling the sacred Vedas, the foundational texts of Hinduism and Brahminism, which served as a core source of esoteric knowledge. This wisdom was passed on through yantras, sacred geometric designs believed to tap into hidden spiritual forces. Initially, yantras were inscribed on cloth or even shirts and worn for protection or placed in the home to ward off evil spirits. These Yants (sacred symbols) became deeply embedded in Khmer culture, spreading across Cambodia, Vietnam, Laos, and Thailand and influencing the spiritual traditions of these regions.

In modern Thai traditions, the term Ruesi is a broad designation, encompassing various practitioners of esoteric sciences, from hermits living in the wilderness to those residing in cities and practicing a wide range of disciplines, including magical tattoos, mantras, yoga, martial arts, meditation, and herbal medicine. Ruesi practices vary widely but share the common thread of pursuing spiritual development and higher wisdom.

Their influence extends deeply into the martial arts of Thailand, particularly Muay Boran, Krabi-Krabong, and Muay Thai. As spiritual mentors, healers, and advisers, the Ruesi played a significant role in the development of martial arts philosophy and training methods.

In Muay Boran, the Ruesi were believed to be teachers to the ancient Nak Muay, imparting both physical training and spiritual knowledge to these warriors. For example, as mentioned earlier, the mythical founder of Muay Lopburi was said to be a Ruesi named Sukatanta. These wise sages taught meditation techniques, breathing exercises, and magical rituals that enhanced a warrior's mental and physical resilience. Rituals such as the Wai Khru, performed to honor teachers and ancestors, reflect the spiritual practices taught by the Ruesi. Fighters often invoke the Ruesi's blessings for protection, mental clarity, and focus before combat. Amulets and sacred Sak Yant tattoos, believed to offer protection and enhance fighting abilities, are also linked to the Ruesi's magical traditions.

A well-known Muay Lopburi technique inspired by the Ruesi is the Ruesi Bod Ya, also known as the "Hermit-Crushing Medicine." This is a powerful jumping elbow strike used to attack the crown of the opponent's head. In Krabi-Krabong, the Ruesi were seen as teachers of ancient combat techniques helping warriors refine their mind-body connection. In modern Muay Thai, the influence of the Ruesi endures not only through sacred rituals like the Wai Khru and Ram Muay but also through Sak Yant tattoos. These sacred tattoos, often inscribed by Ruesi or spiritual masters, are imbued with protective symbols and mantras to enhance strength, courage, and spiritual fortitude, bridging the spiritual power of the Ruesi with the physical demands of Muay Thai.

RUESI DAT TON: SELF-HEALING TRADITIONS

One common example of the ancient Ruesi knowledge was immortalized in the literature of the *Ruesi Dat Ton*, the hermit exercises. This lesser-known facet of traditional Thai culture encompasses breathing exercises, self-mobilization, massage, stretching, dynamic movements, poses, mantras, visualization, and meditation. This exercise system is thought to enhance flexibility, strength, and focus and is believed to be passed down to warriors to strengthen both body and mind, ensuring they remain mentally sharp in battle. It influenced the foundation of traditional Thai massage and uses some of the same techniques also found in Indian hatha yoga and Tibetan yoga traditions.

In 1772, during the reign of King Rama I, the king ordered the knowledge and practices of Ruesi Dat Ton to be documented. The inscriptions at the temple Wat Potharam "Wat Po" (Bangkok) are clear evidence that Ruesi Dat Ton was a traditional Thai self-healing system dating back to this time. Under the royal command, ancient medicine textbooks and sculptures depicting Sen Sib (the energy lines of the body) and various physical postures were restored and preserved at Wat Po. Today, portraits and statues of Ruesi sages performing Ruesi Dat Ton postures are on display at the temple, underscoring the importance of this practice in Thai traditional medicine.

Ruesi Dat Ton is believed to have been developed by Ruesi ascetics as a self-healing practice. The full series of Ruesi Dat Ton inscriptions consists of over eighty postures, ranging from standing poses to lying on the back poses. These postures form a comprehensive system of physical exercises that promote overall well-being. Each posture is designed to balance the body's energy, improve circulation, and enhance both physical and mental health, embodying the holistic approach of traditional Thai medicine.

Due to the complexity of certain postures, the Thai Ministry of Public Health recommends a selection of fifteen poses for general, independent practice. These core poses offer substantial physical and mental health benefits while reducing the risk of injury for beginners and nonexperts.

Practicing these exercises offers numerous positive results, such as enhanced joint mobility, pain alleviation, better digestive and elimination functions, stronger disease resistance, a slowed aging process, and an overall improvement in well-being. It is particularly noted for promoting long life and vitality, especially in the elderly. Many exercises target the spinal column, leg muscles, and lymphatic system, stimulating blood flow and energy throughout the body. It is recognized as an effective practice for healing, improving alignment, and maintaining overall fitness.

NUAD THAI:
THAI MASSAGE AND THE TEN ENERGY LINES

Historians trace the origins of Thai massage (also known as Nuad Thai) back over 2,500 years. It is widely believed that the tradition began with Shivago Komarpaj (also known as Jivaka Komarabhacca), an Indian physician who is revered in Thai culture as the "Father of Thai Medicine."

According to tradition, Shivago was a friend of the Buddha and served as his physician, as well as a healer for the Buddhist monastic community or Sangha. He is said to have developed a healing system that integrated Ayurvedic principles, herbal medicine, and yogic stretching techniques, which later became the foundation of what we know today as traditional Thai massage.

As Buddhist monks traveled from India to Southeast Asia, including present-day Thailand, they brought with them not only the teachings of Buddha but also traditional healing methods, including massage therapy. Thai temples became centers of learning, where monks practiced and preserved various healing arts, including massage, herbal medicine, martial arts, and meditation.

The practice of Nuad Thai became part of the Buddhist monastic tradition, particularly in temples, where monks would use the techniques to heal physical ailments, relieve suffering, and balance the body's energy. This spiritual context is essential to Thai massage, as it is considered both a physical and spiritual practice designed to foster harmony between body, mind, and spirit.

Thai massage continued to evolve over the centuries by integrating influences from neighboring cultures such as China, India, and the Khmer Empire. It developed alongside other aspects of Thai medicine, particularly the ten-energy-line system, called Sen Sib, and a deep understanding of the vital life force energy, called Lom meaning "wind or air." Similar to prana in yoga, qi/ chi in Chinese, or ki in Japanese medicine, the life force energy of Lom is believed to travel along the body's energy pathways, maintaining the body's balance and vitality.

The Ruesi were also instrumental in the development of Thai massage through their Ruesi Dat Ton practices, as this system influenced the stretching, mobility, and pressure-point techniques used in Thai massage today.

In ancient times, Nuad Thai was a crucial element in the physical conditioning and recovery of warriors. As part of regular practice, Thai massage aims to restore balance, relieve pain, improve circulation, and promote overall well-being. The concept of Lom is central to the healing philosophy of traditional Thai massage, underscoring the importance of maintaining the body's internal energy system for optimal health and vitality. This focus on energy flow and body alignment in Thai massage has long complemented the martial disciplines of Muay Boran, Krabi-Krabong, and the modern practice of Muay Thai by helping fighters improve flexibility, recover from injuries, and enhance their overall physical performance.

Thai massage still plays a key role in the lives of Muay Thai fighters today, who rely on it for recovery from injuries, muscle tension relief, and improving flexibility. Prefight massage treatments are common to help athletes enhance mobility, sharpen focus, and warm up, while postfight massages help them recover from the intense physical toll of training and fighting.

LEGENDARY THAI RUESI OR LERSI SAGES

In Thai tradition, there are many révered Ruesi or Lersi figures who hold a special place in folklore and spiritual practices, especially within Thai martial arts. These hermit sages are believed to exist across realms as both supernatural humans and divine, animal-headed beings and are known as "angelic" or "divine" sages. Although much of their legendary lives are shared through oral tradition, folklore, and temple iconography rather than documented historical records, their influence remains strong. These figures are venerated not only for their mystical powers but also for their roles as guides and guardians who offer blessings, protection, and esoteric wisdom.

There are many renowned historical mystical sages, with Phra Lersi Ta Fai and Phra Lersi Phromprasit being particularly revered as embodiments of the spiritual potency attributed to these hermits. Phra Lersi Ta Fai is believed to have attained supernatural powers through his ascetic practices, including the ability to heal, foresee the future and the rise and fall of kings, and provide protection. Depicted with a powerful third eye or "fire eye," symbolizing deep spiritual insight and protective strength, he became a spiritual guide for warriors and kings, offering his wisdom and blessings to those seeking strength and guidance in battle. His tiger-skin cloak is said to have provided him with the power to defeat demons and evil spirits, cementing his status as a guardian of both the physical and spiritual realms. In Thai martial arts, warriors would often invoke his blessings for strength, mental clarity, and resilience. His image and mantras in Sak Yant (sacred tattooing) are believed to bestow physical and spiritual strength. His expertise extends to healing practices, where his knowledge of herbal medicine and energy healing is often called upon for protection and well-being.

Phra Lersi Phromprasit, meanwhile, represents wisdom, magic, moral integrity, and spiritual mentorship. Known as a teacher of magic and moral guidance, his teachings extend to humans, deities, and spirits. His guidance in mystical arts and his emphasis on honor and truthfulness have made him especially revered among scholars and seekers of knowledge. Phra Lersi Phromprasit is believed to have attained a high level of spiritual enlightenment through his meditation and dedication, allowing him to access hidden realms of knowledge and mystical power. As a sage, he was not only a teacher of mystical arts but also a guide for those striving to improve their lives through wisdom and understanding. His legend says that he had the power to grant success in academic endeavors and protection from danger, making him a figure often called upon by scholars, students, and those seeking guidance in difficult times. His protective mantras, used in Sak Yant, are said to grant peace and moral clarity, while his influence remains embedded in Thai healing practices, particularly in herbal medicine and energy healing, to support those seeking wisdom and health.

Among the revered Ruesi, certain figures take inspiration from powerful animals in Thai spiritual culture, like the Tiger, Monkey, and Deer Head Ruesi, each embodying specific qualities vital to both spiritual and martial arts practices.

The Tiger Head Ruesi: Lersi Na Suea is also known as Boromakroo Phu Jao Samingpray. In Thai, his real name and title is "Tan Taw Himawat." He symbolizes strength and protection, inspiring Muay Thai techniques focused on power and aggression, while tiger tattoos associated with him are thought to instill bravery and resilience. In Thai martial arts, his spirit is invoked for mental fortitude and protection. He is frequently honored in Sak Yant practices, where his image and associated mantras are believed to protect fighters and enhance their power, both physically and spiritually. This figure remains an iconic symbol of warrior strength and dedication, deeply connected to Thailand's cultural heritage and the spiritual dimensions of combat.

The Monkey Head Ruesi: Lersi Na Ling is a mythical hermit sage associated with qualities like agility, intelligence, and adaptability. He holds a prominent place in Thai martial arts, especially in Muay Thai and Muay Boran, where his influence is seen in techniques that require agility, evasive movement, and strategic counterattacks. Fighters often seek his blessings to enhance their reflexes, resourcefulness, and mental sharpness. In the Sak Yant tradition, Lersi Na Ling and related mantras are believed to impart to the wearer qualities of adaptability and quick thinking, aiding them in both combat and life challenges. His teachings emphasize not just physical strength but mental resilience and flexibility, reflecting the deeper connection between Thai martial arts and spiritual discipline.

The Deer Head Ruesi: Lersi Na Nuea symbolizes gentleness, vigilance, and spiritual balance in Thai and Southeast Asian traditions. Embodying the qualities of calmness, mindfulness, and careful observation associated with the deer, he teaches patience and heightened awareness. In martial arts, his influence encourages fighters to maintain a calm mind and strategic patience, enabling them to stay composed under pressure. Sak Yant tattoos of Lersi Na Nuea are believed to enhance mental clarity, focus, and spiritual harmony, appealing to those who aspire to embody the deer's peaceful yet alert nature, guided by wisdom and mindfulness.

Their powers, derived from their strict practices, are believed to offer protection, wisdom, and the ability to fulfill wishes. Together, these revered Ruesi figures represent resilience, wisdom, and spiritual guidance. The tradition of praying to these hermits, making offerings, and seeking their blessings is deeply embedded in Thai spiritual practices, and they are frequently depicted in temples and shrines throughout Thailand.

These revered hermits represent the ideal of spiritual discipline, magic, and the power to transcend the ordinary, continuing to play a significant role in Thai religious life and folklore. The yantras (sacred symbols) associated with these Ruesi are often used in Sak Yant tattoos and amulets, imbuing wearers with the protective powers of these sages.

CHAPTER NINE

RITUALS OF PROTECTION: SPELLS, MANTRAS, AND MAGICAL OBJECTS

FINDING PEACE IN THE FACE OF ADVERSITY

While I dedicated myself to training as if my life depended on it, I had realized that my path was not that of a professional fighter. Instead, my goal was to stay sharp and prepared for whatever the universe might throw my way. This commitment to rigorous training became a cornerstone of my life, building both physical resilience and mental strength. As martial artists, we often push ourselves beyond our limits, releasing destructive energy and channeling our fighting spirit into a healthy outlet to enhance greater self-control and discipline. We train not to provoke fights but to handle them wisely if they arise, knowing that the true value of our skills is in how we use them when real-life challenges emerge. However, every trained martial artist eventually faces a situation where their skills are tested outside the controlled environment of the gym. This is where the true value of our training is revealed. The techniques and principles we learn in the gym must translate into real-life situations. This requires not only physical skill but also mental readiness, situational awareness, and the ability to remain calm under pressure.

One of my most memorable experiences of putting this philosophy to the test happened at Alexandra Palace in North London. I was helping a friend sell mixtapes at the Annual Afro Hair & Beauty Show, and after a long day, I was ready to unwind. Drawn by the aroma of Jamaican jerk chicken, I joined the queue at a food stall. While I was waiting, a large man forcefully pushed his way into my place in the queue, sparking a heated exchange. I tried to de-escalate, explaining I just wanted my food after a busy day, but he continued to assert himself, expecting me to back down. I had no intention of provoking a fight, but I wasn't one to allow injustice and was prepared to defend myself if he forced my hand.

The man's aggression escalated, as he challenged me to a fight in front of a gathering crowd. I kept my calm, visualizing potential defenses and counterattacks at close range as the adrenaline began to surge in my body. Some onlookers egged him on while others just watched in shock. My calmness seemed to irritate him, and eventually, he stormed off, only to circle back and attempt a surprise attack from behind. Instinctively, I sensed his approach and sidestepped, his fist grazing past my head. As he stumbled forward, I struck back, landing a punch to his face and a push kick to his chest, sending him tumbling backward.

Unbeknownst to me, he wasn't alone. His friend lunged at me, throwing wild punches, but I dodged and hit him with a hook to the jaw. Another man joined in, attempting to strike, but I slipped his punch and delivered another hit, stunning him. I moved back, fists up, adrenaline pumping, fully prepared to defend myself as I assessed the group. The crowd fell silent as I held my stance, ready for whatever came next.

At that moment, another man approached, warning me that they were part of a group of eight. Although he agreed that the initial aggressor was in the wrong, he noted that if the fight continued, they'd have to back each other up. I didn't care. I was ready to fight. But as I was about to reengage in the impending brawl I heard Arjan Vinny's words echoing in my head: "If you have a way out without fighting, be wise and walk away."

Arjan V often reminded us that in real-life situations, we shouldn't imitate movie legends like Bruce Lee or Tony Jaa taking on multiple opponents at the same time. He advised that if fighting is unavoidable, neutralize the biggest threat brutally first to hopefully deter others. However, he emphasized that fighting should always be a last resort, prioritizing safety and choosing to escape or negotiate whenever possible. In that critical moment, his wisdom resonated with me. Despite my anger and frustration at missing out on my meal and not giving the instigator the beating he seemed to deserve, I chose to walk away, grateful that my training surfaced even in the heat of the moment. Maintaining a steady gaze, I slowly retreated, carrying the weight of unspent energy but also the relief of knowing I had tapped into the true essence of my training.

Magical Spells, Mantras, and Prayers

Ruesi sages and specialist monks skilled in magical practices often reside in temples frequented by martial artists seeking blessings. These monks have typically undergone extensive training in the esoteric aspects of Buddhism, including mystical scriptures detailing the use of magic, spells, prayers, chants, and mantras. Their profound spiritual practices are believed to imbue their magic with powerful energy. Thai martial arts integrates a rich variety of their spells, prayers, and mantras, each with specific purposes that support and empower practitioners on their physical and spiritual journey.

In Thai martial arts, spells, prayers, and mantras are often inscribed on cloth, worn in amulets and talismans, or tattooed on the body, serving as powerful symbols of protection and strength. This variety of magical practices represents the fusion of physical strength and spiritual belief, reflecting the profound connection between martial arts and the cultural and spiritual ethos of Thai culture. These written and spoken words are believed to offer a fighter safety from physical harm and warding off bad luck. By invoking spiritual powers, fighters feel mentally stronger and more focused. This practice honors the traditions and respects the lineage of teachers who have passed down their knowledge from master to student over many generations, offering favor, power, and protection. Fighters and teachers may recite mantras to sharpen focus, enhance resilience, and invoke spiritual protection.

Rituals like the Wai Khru and Ram Muay in Muay Thai blend athleticism, cultural expression, and spiritual practice. Before a match, teachers or coaches will often chant a special mantra while removing the Mongkon, symbolically granting protection, good fortune, and awakening the student's warrior spirit for the challenge ahead. For practitioners, these elements serve as more than just tools for success in combat; they act as connections to heritage, sources of inner strength, and guides for living with honor and spiritual integrity. This reflects the profound integration of Buddhism and traditional Thai beliefs into daily life, especially within the discipline of Muay Thai.

Protective Spells

Protection against physical and spiritual harm is one of the most sought-after forms of magical intervention in Thai martial arts. Fighters often seek blessings from monks who specialize in crafting protective spells. These can take the form of incantations, written scripts, or prayers that are believed to create a metaphysical shield.

Healing Spells

Beyond the physical healing techniques typical to many martial arts, Thai practices often include spells intended to speed recovery, soothe pain, and protect against future injuries. These spells are usually administered by monks or experienced healers who use a combination of prayer, herbal medicine, and sacred inscriptions.

Spells for Success

Success in Thai martial arts isn't seen as merely a result of physical training and strategy. Spells that attract good luck and ensure victory are commonly used. These rituals might involve special ceremonies where offerings are made to spirits or ancestors, accompanied by chanting specific mantras to invoke positive energy and outcomes.

Mantras

Specific prayers, chants, and mantras can be used as part of the Ram Muay and Wai Khru ceremonies invoking support from ancestral spirits and deities. These prayers are typically recited in Pali, an ancient language of Theravada Buddhism, which is deeply respected as the transmitter of ancient knowledge and considered powerful in its own right in Thai culture. A famous Thai Buddhist mantra is NAMO TASSA BHAGAVATO ARAHATO SAMMA SAMBUDDHASSA, a traditional Buddhist salutation that translates to "I pay homage to the Blessed One, the Worthy One, the Fully Enlightened One." Often recited three times, this phrase is used as an expression of deep respect for the Buddha and is typically spoken by a layperson, a warrior, a teacher, a monk, or a nun.

This salutation is central to the Buddhist practice of taking refuge in the Triple Gem or Three Jewels: the Buddha, the Dhamma (teachings), and the Sangha (community). Taking refuge in the Three Jewels formally initiates an individual into Buddhist practice, marking a commitment to following the Buddha's path. The word-by-word meaning of the phrase is:

Namo: "I pay homage"

Tassa: "to him"

Bhagavato: "to the Exalted One"

Arahato: "to The Worthy One"

Samma Sambuddhassa: "to The Fully Enlightened One"

It's a way for Muay Thai practitioners to connect with the teachings of the Buddha for guidance, protection, and spiritual strength before engaging in their fights.

Another Thai mantra is:

GAM BAAN NAK MUEN

This roughly translates to "ten thousand pounds of strength" or "a weight of ten thousand." The expression typically signifies an immense force and can be used to focus a fighter's mind for exceptional power, resilience, or fortitude.

Here are a few examples of English mantras that Western Muay Thai fighters might use to build mental focus and resilience:

I CAN DO THIS, NO MATTER THE CHALLENGE, I'M READY
FOR WAR.

THE HARDER THE CHALLENGE, THE HARDER I FIGHT.

NEVER QUIT, NEVER SURRENDER, I WILL RISE TRIUMPHANT!

BREATHE, BELIEVE, ACHIEVE.

Prayers

Teachers and students often use personal prayers to help ground,
focus, and empower students during training or fighting. Here
are a couple of examples I was taught by Arjan Vinny and others
I've learned and developed on my journey.

May the great spirit who guides all warriors, grant me
strength to face this challenge with courage, focus,
and honor. Protect me from harm, help me to remain
calm and clearheaded, and guide my actions with wisdom, strength, and skill. May I honor my training, my
coaches, and the journey that brought me here.

May my student be fully empowered in all aspects of
their training. May they be centered within their highest abilities, competing with strength and focus. May
they honor their training, their club, their teacher, and
themselves in all they do. May both my student and
their opponent emerge unharmed. May my student
overcome all challenges and rise victorious.

Reciting prayers and mantras before a fight helps fighters center
themselves, reduce anxiety, and build confidence. The rhythmic

repetition of mantras, in particular, can cultivate mental clarity, reinforce breathing techniques, and calm prefight nerves, allowing fighters to enter the ring with focus and determination.

This mental discipline is essential in Muay Thai, where maintaining composure under pressure can be the decisive factor between victory and defeat.

INSTRUMENTS OF MAGIC

The belief in the power of charms, amulets, and talismans stretches back to early human cultures, arising from the idea that certain objects, whether found or crafted, carry unique meanings. These items were believed to hold spiritual significance, offering protection, luck, or strength to those who possessed them. In Thai culture, fighters, teachers, and everyday people often incorporate charms, amulets, and talismans into their attire for combat, ceremonies, or daily activities. These revered objects are potent spiritual tools imbued with distinct magical properties and intentions. Each item is carefully crafted and sanctified to serve a unique purpose: a charm draws in good fortune; an amulet provides protection from harm; and a talisman channels a specific benefit or strength to its owner. The lines can also sometimes be blurred as some objects offer both luck and protection and special benefits to the holder.

Often custom-made, these pieces are individually anointed and consecrated to align with the wearer's needs, embodying a personal connection for their intended purpose. Whether worn as jewelry, sewn into clothing, or carried discreetly, these enchanted items hold significant importance. They are believed to provide protection, bring good fortune, and instill a deeper sense of confidence, allowing individuals to face challenges with more security derived from their magical, spiritual, and protective objects.

Charms

These magical items are small, sacred, and decorative objects believed to provide specific benefits, such as luck, love, protection, or prosperity. Charms often come in various forms—like small cloth bundles; metal, stone, or wooden objects; or tiny statues that may include specific images or symbols like animals, deities, or inscriptions. Charms often have a single focus or purpose with specific intentions and can be carried in a pocket or purse or even be placed in a home or vehicle. They are used to attract good fortune, bring luck, and prevent misfortune.

Amulets

Unlike charms, which are often kept in a pocket or placed in a specific location, amulets are typically worn around the neck and are believed to provide broader benefits, such as overall protection or spiritual empowerment. Thai amulets are small, intricately crafted objects, usually depicting the Buddha or a respected monk, warrior, or animal, and are often crafted from materials such as wood, stone, or metal. They are typically worn as pendants, embodying a blend of supernatural beliefs and Thai cultural values. These amulets are valued for their believed powers, connecting to themes like farming traditions, family loyalty, martial lineage, gratitude, and cultural history.

Amulets are considered powerful sources of protection and strength, often worn by Muay Thai fighters around their necks or placed on their Mongkon before the fight for spiritual support. There are many different types of these sacred amulets, each believed to provide a protective shield against negative energies, empowering wearers with resilience and safeguarding them from harm. Here's an overview of some of the most revered amulets for warriors:

The Phra Somdej Amulet: Known as "The King of Amulets," Phra Somdej is believed to offer supreme protection, good fortune, and enhanced resilience. Crafted from a unique blend of sacred materials, including oil, soil, pollen, incense ashes, temple dirt, and relics from revered monks—such as a monk's hair, pieces of the holy robe, and other revered relics—it typically depicts a seated Buddha or bodhisattva and is encased in silver or other protective metals, embodying peace, resilience, and spiritual protection. This revered amulet is cherished for its deep spiritual significance, believed to bring protection, health, better relationships, peace, power, and good luck to those who wear it.

The Tiger Amulet: Symbolizing strength, courage, and resilience, this is a popular choice for fighters and people seeking to embody the fearless spirit of the tiger. Believed to instill bravery and offer protection in challenging situations, this amulet serves as a symbol of empowerment in combat and daily life. One of Thailand's most revered monks, Luang Phor Pern of Wat Bang Phra, a temple in Nakhon Pathom province, became renowned for his mastery of incantations, amulets, and Sak Yant featuring tiger imagery. During his lifetime, Luang Phor Pern attracted a large following, with devotees flocking daily to Wat Bang Phra to receive his blessings. The Tiger (Sua) Amulet inspired by his teachings is cherished for imbuing wearers with fearlessness, strength, and resilience, making it a respected emblem of empowerment and protection.

Legend has it that during a spiritual journey through the hills, Luang Phor Pern encountered a fierce tiger. While his followers fled, he calmly sat and began to meditate, prompting the tiger to leave peacefully. News of this incident spread quickly, and soon, people from regions plagued by tiger attacks flocked to Wat Bang Phra seeking Sak Yant tattoos and protective amulets. According to oral tradition, remarkably no one bearing his blessed tattoos or amulets was ever harmed by a tiger. Luang Phor Pern passed away in 2002 at seventy-nine, after fifty-four years in the monkhood. His mummified body remains visible in a glass case at Wat Bang Phra, where a large statue of him also stands overlooking the temple grounds.

The Hanuman Amulet: Representing strength, resilience, and loyalty, this is a favored choice for those seeking courage and the ability to overcome adversity. Drawing from the legendary story of the monkey god Hanuman in the Ramakien, this amulet embodies agility, quick thinking, and invincibility. Known for his ability to be revived with just a breath of wind, Hanuman's resilience inspires Muay Thai fighters, who believe the amulet will give them his fighting abilities but also help them rise again if they happen to be knocked down. The amulet is also popular among soldiers, police, and frontline workers, enhancing their bravery and unwavering determination. In these amulets Hanuman is often depicted wielding a victory flag or weapons, underscoring his role as a divine warrior and protector.

Hanuman is one of Thailand's most revered symbols and also among the most sought-after amulets. These amulets are believed to offer their wearer strength, skill, and success in all areas of their life, as well as protection from harm, evil spirits, and negative forces, making them one of the most cherished amulets across Thailand.

The Turtle Amulet (Pha Ya Tow): Known for bringing good fortune, protection, and longevity, this amulet is treasured for its grounding influence and endurance. The turtle, symbolizing persistence and forward movement, embodies a prosperous life that never retreats. The amulet typically takes the shape of a turtle and is adorned with an image of Phra Sangkachai (the Laughing Buddha) smiling on the front to impart happiness to its wearer. On the reverse side, a powerful Sak Yant is often inscribed, thought to grant success, resilience in facing obstacles, and protective energies.

The amulet's power is said to deepen with regular wear, echoing the turtle's slow, steady path and reminding the wearer that patience yields the best rewards. Often made from wood and encased in silver and gold, the Turtle Amulet stands as a symbol of patience and endurance—qualities revered in Muay Thai and essential for lasting success and resilience.

Thao Wessuwan Amulet: Depicting the powerful guardian and leader of all ghosts and demons, this amulet is highly valued for its protective abilities and its potential to attract financial gain. Thao Wessuwan, often shown wielding a truncheon or krabong, is believed to possess the power to hurl it through the air, cracking the heads of thousands of ghosts with a single throw. His compassionate nature prevents him from completely destroying these spirits, instead only wounding them as a lesson.

Thao Wessuwan's image is widely used in Thailand as a protective symbol, often placed on cloth and put above doorways to keep away thieves and malevolent spirits. Large statues of him stand guard at the entrances of numerous temples across the country, and an impressive figure of Thao Wessuwan presides over the departures area at Bangkok's Suvarnabhumi Airport.

It is a highly popular amulet believed to help those seeking protection from ghosts, demons, and physical harm. It is also a favorite among businesspeople, believed to draw financial prosperity and abundance. For Muay Thai fighters, the Thao Wessuwan amulet offers both spiritual protection and an aura of resilience, appealing to those who seek physical safety and personal success.

The Khun Paen Amulet: This is one of Thailand's most famous and revered talismans, deeply rooted in Thai folklore and spiritual tradition. Named after the legendary warrior Khun Paen, renowned for his skills in martial arts, charm, and mastery of mystical arts, this amulet is believed to embody his qualities of bravery, charisma, and protective power.

Traditionally, the Khun Paen amulet is worn to attract love, enhance personal charm, and inspire admiration, courage, and resilience. It is said to help Muay Thai practitioners to stay focused, brave, and safe from harm. Believed to enhance personal magnetism and fortitude, it offers wearers a spiritual shield to endure and overcome adversity.

Many Khun Paen amulets feature the figure of Khun Paen seated in a meditative or protective posture, sometimes surrounded by smaller spirits or symbols of protection. These amulets may also include mantras or sacred inscriptions, believed to amplify their powers. Crafted from sacred materials like temple clay, relics, or even the ashes of revered monks, the amulet's potency is enhanced by the blessings and rituals performed by skilled monks during its creation.

Khun Paen amulets are highly sought after by Muay Thai fighters, businesspeople, and anyone who desires to embody strength, charm, and resilience in life, staying connected to the enduring legacy of one of Thailand's most celebrated historical figures.

These amulets offer much more than mere decoration; they are cherished for their spiritual strength and resilience, bolstering both mental and physical well-being. Each amulet embodies a distinctive fusion of artistry, symbolism, and spiritual energy, selected by wearers for particular attributes that enhance their intentions and journey, especially within the rigorous practice of Muay Thai.

Talismans of Power and Protection

In Thai culture, particularly within Thai martial arts, talismans are considered to augment specific traits in individuals. In Muay Thai, they are thought to increase a fighter's inner strength, courage, resilience, and agility. These talismans are thought to channel spiritual power for personal enhancement. These objects are often carved from wood, stone, or metal and are believed to have magical properties. They are often inscribed with sacred texts or symbols to amplify personal abilities, attract positive influences, and provide the wearer with spiritual power or success. Even many Thai amulets can also function as talismans. The distinction between the two often blurs, especially in Thai spiritual practice, where an amulet may be consecrated not only for protection—its role as an amulet—but also to attract specific qualities, strengths, or benefits to its wearer—which is characteristic of a talisman. Many aspects of a Muay Thai fighter's attire can be imbued with magical qualities from talismans. Key examples include:

Mongkon (Sacred Headband): Often blessed by a monk or Kru, imbued with hidden sacred writings or symbols, and serves to elevate focus, mental clarity, and spiritual strength. It's worn during the Wai Khru ceremony to connect with ancestors and spirits, believed to bring inner power, bravery, and honor.

Pra Jiad (Armbands): These armbands are commonly made from cloth belonging to a fighter's family or from items significant to them. Infused with intention, the Pra Jiad is considered a source of inner resilience, helping fighters draw upon strength and endurance in the ring. They are also believed to bring fortune, but more importantly, are meant to boost a fighter's spirit.

Sak Yant Tattoos: Many sacred tattoos are believed to function as talismans, particularly those focused on amplifying personal attributes. For example, the Yant Suea (Tiger Yant) represents courage, strength, and the fighting spirit, while the Yant Hanuman invokes fearlessness and invincibility. These tattoos are custom made and blessed by a monk or tattoo master, who imbues them with spiritual power to enhance a fighter's capabilities.

Kuman Thong: Originating from Khun Paen's legendary lore, the Kuman Thong (Golden Child) is a talisman crafted to invoke the spirit of a protective child. Though more rare among fighters, some wear it as a charm to bring guidance and strength in dangerous situations.

Takrut Scrolls: These small sacred scrolls are typically made of metal, palm leaf, or cloth and inscribed with sacred texts, mantras, or prayers. These elongated scrolls, often tied around the neck, wrist, or waist with a cord, offer specific spiritual benefits to their wearers. As well as their distinctive scroll shape, they often incorporate elements like engraved gemstones, statues, coins, drawings, pendants, rings, plants, and even small animal symbols. They may also feature inscribed words or spells intended to attract good fortune or repel negative energies.

Takrut scrolls hold special significance for Muay Thai fighters, soldiers, and those facing high-stakes environments, as they are believed to enhance courage, resilience, and physical strength. Each Takrut is meticulously crafted, with monks or Ruesi reciting spells or blessing the scroll as part of its creation. The inscriptions may be personalized or follow traditional incantations designed to channel protective forces or increase mental clarity. This ritualistic process elevates the Takrut from a simple accessory to a powerful spiritual tool, revered for its reputed ability to strengthen the wearer's resolve, focus, and fortitude.

Each talisman in Thai culture and Thai martial arts is more than a symbolic item. They are believed to connect fighters to a lineage of spiritual practice, instilling inner strength and qualities essential for success in both combat and life.

CHAPTER TEN

MAGICAL TATTOOS: STRENGTH AND PROTECTION

RETURNING TO THE SOURCE

For my thirtieth birthday, I gave myself the ultimate gift: a month-long trip to Thailand. Being able to return to the source of my martial art had been a dream of mine since I began practicing Muay Thai at the age of sixteen, but it took fourteen years before I finally made it happen. I was eager to immerse myself in Muay Thai and Muay Boran training and dive deeper into Thai history and culture. The twelve-hour flight was filled with excitement and anticipation. This was my martial homecoming—a return to where it all began. Despite my anticipation, I had no idea how profoundly this experience would impact me.

Traveling alone, I followed the advice of Arjan V, who had recommended I first pay my respects to his teacher, Grand Master Woody in Bangkok. Associate Senior Grand Master Chinawut Sirisompan, also known as Grand Master Woody, led the Kru Muay Thai Association (KMA) dedicated to preserving and promoting traditional Thai martial arts. He welcomed me warmly and introduced me to Assistant Grand Master Suphan Chabiarum, known as Kru Supan. Despite a face battle-scarred from over 300 fights, Kru Supan was a joyful and knowledgeable teacher. Training with him daily in Bangkok for a week felt like a year's worth of progress back home. Kru Supan didn't just take me at face value; he thoroughly evaluated my existing knowledge and systematically introduced me to new punches, elbows, knees, and kick forms, constantly refining and raising my skills. His guidance elevated my understanding of Muay Boran and Muay Thai techniques, pushing my practice to new heights.

As I explored Bangkok, I visited palaces, temples, floating markets, modern shopping centers, and popular tourist spots. Bangkok was a city full of life, a vibrant mix of tradition and modernity, with sleek architecture catering to a fast-paced, globalized world. The food was exceptional, blending sweet and spicy flavors in perfectly cooked meat and vegetable dishes. It was a sensory experience that left a lasting impression.

After Bangkok, I traveled to the Thai island of Phuket, where I immersed myself in the local culture and experienced the vibrant fights in Muay Thai at Phuket Stadium. The energy was electric, with gamblers, locals, and tourists captivated by the display of skill and courage. That night, I met a local fighter who offered me private training sessions for a fee. The next day, I showed up at his small studio gym and was introduced to what I know now as "farang training," a style tailored for foreign tourists—a less technical but explosive workout. It was intense, filled with hard pad work and fitness drills that tested my stamina, strength, and endurance. The focus was more on building power and conditioning than on deep technical knowledge, but it was a valuable experience, nonetheless.

Seeking more technical training, I followed a recommendation and went to the island of Koh Samui to visit Lamai Muay Thai, where I was unexpectedly reunited with my first-ever Muay Thai trainer, Ralph Beale. Unbeknownst to me, Ralph had established his gym there, and this serendipitous homecoming marked the start of an intense two-week training schedule. I lived and trained like a professional fighter, pushing myself with two-hour sessions twice a day, six days a week. Mornings began with a 7 a.m. run, followed by Muay Thai drills, bag work, strength training, and technical practice. Afternoons were free for rest, exploring the island, or relaxing at the beach before another rigorous session at 5 p.m. The relentless routine pushed my body to its limits, cutting weight and forging mental and physical strength. The coaches, many of whom were former champions, were friendly and highly skilled, making the experience both challenging and deeply rewarding.

As I journeyed across Thailand, I also experienced some of the nightlife, which was heavily influenced by tourism. Bars, pleasure houses, and nightclubs lined the streets, offering foreigners an escape into indulgence. This vibrant scene was a stark contrast to the calm, reflective Buddhist temples, the disciplined gym environments, and the pristine tropical landscapes. The juxtaposition of these two sides of Thailand was striking, revealing a complex balance between tradition and modernity, the sacred and the profane.

I noticed another contrast between Thai and Western fighters. While Western fighters often displayed overt aggression and competed for bragging rights, Thai fighters demonstrated incredible skill without arrogance. The warrior's code in Thailand, so deeply rooted in Buddhist values, emphasized humility, respect, and dedication.

My travels through Thailand enriched me as a martial artist and as a person. The entire month felt like five years of training back home. It wasn't just about honing my skills as a fighter; it was also a profound experience that enriched my life.

My visit to Thailand went beyond physical training and learning about the rich history and culture surrounding Muay Thai; it taught me the importance of balancing my higher and lower states of being. I understood that true mastery in Muay Thai isn't only about physical skill; it's about harmonizing my higher qualities, such as compassion, integrity, discipline, and humility, with my instinctual drives for strength, determination, survival, and resilience. Embracing these values revealed a deeper dimension to the art, enhancing my awareness and expanding my journey of self-discovery and growth. These key lessons continue to shape my approach to life both as a student and teacher.

Sacred Markings: Sak Yant Tattoos

The word *Sak* means "to tap" or "to tattoo," while *Yant* is derived from the Sanskrit word *yantra* meaning "instrument," "device," or "tool." In a spiritual context, it refers to a geometric diagram or mystical symbol used as a tool for meditation, focus, and harnessing spiritual energy. In essence, *Sak Yant* can be translated to mean the "sacred instrument" or "tool of sacred geometrical designs."

In Thai martial arts, Ruesi sages and specialist monks would pass down their esoteric knowledge to warriors, including the inking of sacred tattoos or Sak Yants believed to carry protective spells and serve as embodied talismans. These practices were believed to strengthen both mind and body, protecting warriors from harm and spiritual threats. The magical tattoos commonly worn by fighters are said to originate from the Ruesi, enhancing the wearer's resilience and abilities in battle.

The Ruesi teachings emphasize that true martial mastery comes from the balance of mind, body, and spirit, highlighting the deep connection between spirituality and Thai martial arts. These ancient sages often retreated deep into forests where they spent their time in meditation and self-discipline. Through their rigorous practices, it is said that they unlocked the knowledge of the physical and spiritual universe, understanding the sacred geometrical designs of creation that are known as yantras. These yantras are believed to tap into hidden spiritual forces of the universe and provide protection from harm.

Yantras, originally inscribed on cloth or clothing, were used across Southeast Asia for spiritual protection and to ward off negative influences or spirits. Over time, these sacred symbols became widely incorporated into Khmer culture and, subsequently, into the broader spiritual practices of Southeast Asia, including Cambodia, Vietnam, Laos, and Siam (modern-day Thailand), where they are now known as Yants.

As the kingdom of Siam developed, Yants became a fundamental part of Siamese spiritual life. They were integrated into various religious and cultural practices, offering protection, empowerment, and spiritual connection. In ancient Siam, these symbols evolved into the practice of Sak Yant, the sacred tattoo tradition that remains popular to this day. This transition from cloth to skin reflects the deep spiritual significance of yantras in Thai culture, where they continue to serve as powerful sources of protection, good fortune, and spiritual strength for those who wear them.

Traditionally Sak Yants are applied to the skin in Thailand and other parts of Southeast Asia. They are created using a specialized bamboo rod or steel needle wielded by a highly respected spiritual practitioner—often a Buddhist monk, Arjan (a master teacher), or Ruesi (hermit sage). This unique tattooing technique involves hand-tapping the needle to insert ink under the skin, a method that allows for more intricate and precise designs than machine-based tattooing.

The process of receiving a Sak Yant is viewed as a spiritual rite of passage. Before the tattooing begins, a ritual is conducted to honor the spiritual lineage of the tattoo design and to call upon protective blessings. During the tattooing, the Arjan, monk, or Ruesi often chants mantras, invoking the tattoo's protective powers as they inscribe the sacred designs. Each Sak Yant is more than just a symbol: it is believed to carry specific powers, such as protection, strength, good fortune, or spiritual guidance. After the tattoo is completed, a blessing or prayer is offered to seal its spiritual power. The wearer is often required to follow certain moral precepts, similar to Buddhist teachings, as the power of the Sak Yant is said to depend on adherence to righteous living.

In the world of Thai martial arts, Sak Yant has a long-standing tradition, sought by both ancient warriors and modern fighters for protection and power in battle. These tattoos are believed to enhance mental and spiritual strength, crucial for the psychological demands of combat, while also connecting fighters to their cultural heritage and martial tradition.

Sak Yant tattoos are not just protective amulets; they are imbued with spells believed to offer invincibility in battle, enhanced strength, protection from harm, and the attraction of good fortune. They also embody a deep commitment to discipline, honor, and ethical integrity.

Sak Yant designs vary widely, including geometric shapes, animal figures, sacred texts, and Buddhist or Hindu deities, each with unique meanings and spiritual significance. A genuine Sak Yant starts with a foundational design template, which the Sak Yant master then customizes by modifying the spell to align with the individual's unique intentions and desires. This is why an authentic Sak Yant cannot be created by a standard tattoo artist unfamiliar with the magical script who merely replicates designs and mantras from online sources. Without specific knowledge, there's a risk of accidentally inscribing a blessing meant for someone else.

Each Sak Yant symbol is imbued with spells for protection, strength, and courage, tailored by the Sak Yant master to meet the wearer's unique needs. Variations of each design emphasize different aspects of empowerment, from protection to personal growth. I have included some drawings of Sak Yant designs as references to reflect the unique forms and symbolism. However, since these designs were not made by a Sak Yant Arjan (master) or monk, they do not carry the spiritual or magical power of a traditional Sak Yant. While these designs are inspired by authentic symbols, they should not be mistaken for consecrated Sak Yants. For those seeking a true Sak Yant, I encourage you to connect with a properly trained Sak Yant Arjan or monk in Thailand who practices this sacred tradition.

Geometric Sak Yants

These sacred Sak Yant designs are usually based on yantras, the sacred geometric patterns believed to channel spiritual energy. These tattoos are often created with intricate symmetry and balance, reflecting universal harmony and spiritual protection. Some popular geometric Sak Yants designs include:

Gao Yord (Nine Peaks): This tattoo features the nine peaks of Mount Sumeru, a sacred mountain in Hinduism, Jainism, and Buddhism. It symbolizes spiritual ascension and is associated with protection, success, and good fortune.

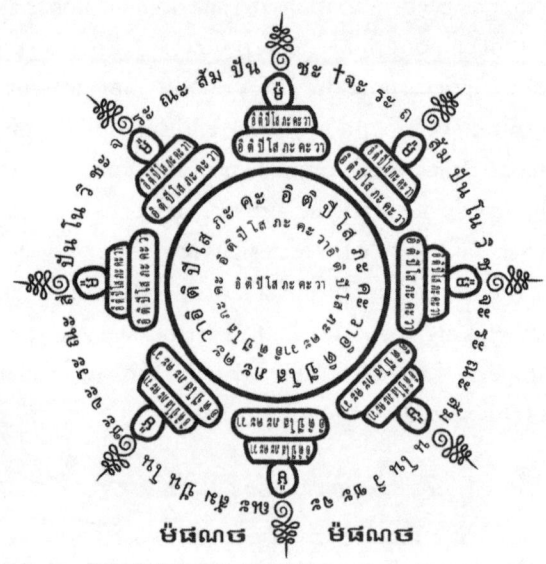

Paed Tidt (Eight Directions): Composed of eight directional lines radiating from a central point, this symbol represents protection in all directions, shielding the wearer from negative forces. It is believed to protect the wearer from harm traveling from all directions no matter where they are.

Unalome (Spiritual Path): Known in Thailand, India, and Nepal for centuries, this design represents the journey to enlightenment and is often called the "Buddha eye" or "third eye of the Buddha." Its spirals symbolize life's struggles, while the straight line above signifies clarity and spiritual awakening, guiding the wearer on a path of inner peace and insight.

Animal Sak Yants

Sak Yants based on animals tend to embody the specific qualities admired in Thai spiritual and martial traditions, such as strength, courage, intelligence, and agility. These designs are believed to transfer the attributes of the animal to the wearer, making them popular among fighters, athletes, and those seeking protection. They can often combine the powers of deities who also embody these qualities. Some popular animal Sak Yants designs include:

Suea (Tiger) represents strength, power, and authority, often chosen by those seeking confidence and courage. The twin tiger design, in particular, is believed to double these protective attributes.

Hanuman, inspired by the mythological monkey god from the Ramakien, symbolizing strength in adversity, loyalty, agility, and fearlessness. It is favored by Muay Thai fighters for its blessings of resilience and success in battle. It is popular among those who wish to harness agility, quick thinking, and the legendary resilience of Hanuman.

Elephant: Representing the Hindu elephant deity Ganesha, named Erawan in Thai, this is the revered three-headed elephant god of wisdom, strength, and removal of obstacles. Favored by business owners, artists, and those facing significant challenges, this Sak Yant is believed to bestow prosperity, resilience, stability, wisdom, and the empowering qualities of the elephant or deity.

Sacred Texts (Mantras)

Sak Yants that feature sacred texts or mantras are believed to carry great power and protection. The majority of Sak Yants incorporate sacred scripts (Khmer or Pali text). These scripts, spells, or prayers are often chanted during the tattooing process, invoking the power of the words to protect, guide, and empower the wearer. Some popular sacred text include:

Hah Taew (Five Lines): Consisting of five vertical lines, each representing a distinct blessing or protection, this is one of the most revered Sak Yant designs. The five lines are considered to shield the bearer from evil spirits, misfortune, and bad luck, embodying a powerful and multifaceted spiritual protection.

Yant Metta Maha Niyom: In Thai culture, *Metta* and *Maha Niyom* mean "Great Loving-Kindness and Popularity." The phrase is deeply rooted in Buddhist teachings, emphasizing universal compassion and goodwill toward others. It is specifically intended to enhance the wearer's personal charm, likability, and social appeal, creating a magnetic quality that draws others to them and makes people more inclined to offer kindness and assistance.

Sak Yants Representing Deities and Sages

Sak Yants featuring Buddhist and Hindu deities, as well as revered sages, are seen as powerful symbols of divine protection, wisdom, and spiritual empowerment. Each of these sacred tattoos connects the wearer to Thailand's rich cultural and spiritual heritage, embodying the gifts, powers, and virtues of these esteemed figures.

Yant Prajao Ha Pra Ong (Five Buddhas): Offering the ultimate protection, spiritual enlightenment, and guidance, the five buddhas represent the enlightened beings of the five directions—north, east, south, west, and center—who each offer blessings of good luck, love, and charm, shielding the wearer from harm and fostering inner growth.

Yant Ruesi—The Wise Sage: Designs incorporating the image of a Ruesi represent the wearer's desire for spiritual wisdom, healing abilities, and protection from evil. It connects the individual with the ancient knowledge of the Ruesi sages, encouraging spiritual growth and self-discipline.

Pha Ram Shooting Arrows (Pha Ram): Inspired by the hero of the Ramakien, this Sak Yant depicts Pha Ram riding atop a naga (the divine serpent) and releasing arrows, symbolizing focused strength and protection in challenging times. This design is believed to bring resilience, authority, and success, offering powerful protection, invincibility, and victory over adversaries. Often chosen by those who seek Pha Ram's legendary courage, honor, and determination, this design represents triumph against obstacles and the ability to lead with strength and integrity.

There exists a vast array of Sak Yants, each with unique symbolism and meaning, offering countless combinations that resonate with deep spiritual empowerment. These designs have evolved over centuries, each embodying powerful blessings and spiritual intentions rooted in ancient traditions.

The spiritual legacy of the Ruesi sages and their sacred yantras endures through the Sak Yant tradition, with ceremonies still regularly held in temples like Wat Bang Phra, where both Buddhist and Ruesi influences are honored. Sak Yant continues as a vibrant, living tradition, drawing Muay Thai fighters, people in risky professions, and everyday individuals alike who seek these tattoos for diverse reasons, such as invoking luck, love, and resilience or to cultivate qualities like confidence and mindfulness. However, as Sak Yant has gained international popularity, there has been a rise in nonauthentic versions created by tattoo artists who lack the spiritual training required to apply them correctly. Unlike the traditional Sak Yant bestowed with blessings, protective spells, and spiritual energy, these decorative imitations lack the profound ceremonial essence and cultural connection of the originals.

Still the ongoing popularity of Sak Yant reflects how this ancient wisdom resonates in contemporary life, preserving a powerful symbol of spiritual protection, personal transformation, and Thai cultural identity across generations.

SAK YANT TEMPLES

There are several places in Thailand where one can receive a Sak Yant tattoo from traditional temples to private studios. Across Bangkok and other parts of the country, many temples are known for offering Sak Yant tattoos, often performed by an Arjan or monk. These tattoos are typically provided on a donation basis, with some temples offering them free of charge or for a nominal fee. However, among all Sak Yant locations, Wat Bang Phra in Nakhon Pathom province stands out as the most renowned site—a temple attracting both Thai locals and international visitors.

Wat Bang Phra, established centuries ago during the Ayutthaya period, initially served as a prominent center for Buddhist learning and meditation. It gained wide recognition in the twentieth century as a center for Sak Yant tattooing largely due to the influence of Luang Phor Pern, a revered monk who served there. Known for his deep spiritual insight and mastery of yantra tattooing, Luang Phor Pern applied his expertise to imbue followers with protection, strength, and good fortune through sacred tattoos. He introduced unique Yant designs believed to offer powerful protection and luck, connecting ancient designs and mantras with modern applications.

The temple remains a major destination for those seeking the spiritual benefits of Sak Yant. Each year, Wat Bang Phra holds a Wai Khru ceremony where hundreds of devotees come to receive new tattoos or have existing ones recharged with spiritual energy. The ceremony includes ritual chants and blessings, and participants often enter trancelike states believed to represent the embodiment of the animals or deities featured in their tattoos, reinforcing the tattoo's spiritual power.

Today, Wat Bang Phra has achieved global renown, with countless international visitors, including celebrities, traveling to experience its Sak Yant tradition. The temple continues to uphold high standards in training monks in yantra tattooing, preserving this ancient art while adapting it to contemporary life. Acting as a cultural bridge, Wat Bang Phra allows people worldwide to engage with Thailand's spiritual heritage, sharing the profound experience of Sak Yant as a timeless source of spiritual connection and protection.

SAK YANT CEREMONIES

A Sak Yant ceremony is typically conducted by a Ruesi, Arjan, or Buddhist monk who has been trained in the sacred art of Sak Yant and its mystical symbols, prayers, and invocations. The ceremony begins with the recipient kneeling respectfully before the monk or Ruesi, who often performs a prayer or chant to invoke protection and blessings. The client makes an offering to the Sak Yant master, which can include a flower, candle, incense, money, Thai rum, cigarettes, or traditional Thai chewing gum. The offering shows respect to the master and the tradition and indicates that the client is ready to follow the rules of the Sak Yant. The monk uses a long, bamboo needle or pointed metal rod to apply the tattoo. The ink may include various sacred components, such as herbs, charred oils, or snake venom, which are believed to imbue the tattoo with magical properties.

As the monk carefully etches the intricate design into the skin, he recites ancient prayers and mantras in Pali or Khmer, infusing the tattoo with its intended power, whether for protection, strength, confidence, or charisma. The most popular designs often feature animal symbols, such as tigers or mythical creatures, along with sacred geometrical shapes, each carrying specific spiritual meanings.

Upon completion, the Ruesi, Arjan, or monk blesses the tattoo, chanting a final incantation to awaken the tattoo's power. Some believe that the recipient may experience a surge of energy or spiritual transformation as the tattoo's power integrates into their being. Traditionally, the ceremony concludes with the monk giving guidance on how to maintain the tattoo's blessings, often advising on ethical conduct and rules to preserve the tattoo's spiritual potency, such as refraining from certain actions or foods.

A Sak Yant ceremony is a profound experience that goes far beyond the physical tattoo, as it connects the recipient to a lineage of spiritual and protective energy, serving as a lifelong reminder of their journey, purpose, and the guidance of ancient Thai wisdom.

RULES OF THE SAK YANT

Created by the Ruesi, Arjan, or Buddhist monk who performs the ceremony, Sak Yant tattoo rules are intended to uphold the tattoo's spiritual power and protective qualities. These rules form a code of ethical conduct leading the wearer toward a mindful and virtuous life:

The Sak Yant is meant to serve as a spiritual guide in a person's life and should only be undertaken by those committed to leading a virtuous life. The magical power within the Sak Yant relies on the quality of a person's thoughts and actions to remain strong. The accompanying rules are intended to emphasize key principles that help keep this spiritual energy active and aligned. Though the rules may vary slightly depending on the type of Sak Yant, the teachings of the Sak Yant master, or the specific temple, some of the most widely observed include:

- Do not kill any living creature.
- Do not steal or lie.
- Be faithful in relationships.
- Avoid intoxication.
- Do not speak ill of family or elders.
- Do not desire or pursue another person's lover or spouse.

These rules reflect a commitment to respect, kindness, and mindfulness, which are core principles of Thai Buddhist culture. For many practitioners, following these guidelines is not only essential to preserve the tattoo's power but also a way to live in alignment with the spiritual virtues that Sak Yants embody. If a wearer violates these rules, it is customary to return to the monk or master who created the tattoo for a blessing to restore the Sak Yant's spiritual power. This reblessing serves as a reminder of the tattoo's purpose and a reaffirmation of the wearer's commitment to leading an ethical life.

CHAPTER ELEVEN

MUAY THAI SPIRITUAL PHILOSOPHY

FROM NOVICE TO MASTERY

I've had the privilege to visit Thailand many times, each trip deepening my understanding of the sports of Muay Thai, Muay Boran, and Krabi-Krabong, as well as Thai culture overall. My journeys have included everything from personal training to intensive fight camps to supporting and cornering for fighters to compete at the International and Thai Martial Arts Games in Bangkok.

Among my many experiences, some of my most cherished have been meeting and training with Muay Thai legends like Saenchai, Buakaw Banchamek, and Yodsanklai Fairtex. These encounters not only deepened my understanding of fighting techniques but also offered invaluable insights into the mindset and character of some of the sport's greatest fighters of our time. While watching them in the ring was undoubtedly a gift in itself, one of the most memorable moments was sparring with Saenchai and participating in a few personal training sessions with him at the Yokkao Training Center in Bangkok. During our sparring session, I witnessed firsthand the extraordinary precision of his timing and his remarkable ability to read the flow of the fight in the blink of an eye. His playful and relaxed style elevated the concept of finding peace in the face of adversity to an entirely new level.

Over the years, my training has been shaped by the structured grading system founded by Grand Master Woody and the Kru Muay Thai Association and developed by Arjan Vinny, a system dedicated to preserving and advancing traditional Thai martial arts. The rankings, from Khan 1 to Khan 19, cover foundational skills through the highest levels of mastery. Reaching Khan 10 is comparable to a black belt in other martial arts, while Khan 12 qualifies one as a teacher (Kru). In London, Arjan V mentored me through our grading system, and at the age of thirty he honored me with the title of assistant Kru (teacher) at the 11th Khan, recognizing my dedication and my skill as a martial artist and as a teacher.

At thirty-three, during a training tour in Thailand with Arjan V, I reached a significant milestone. I had the chance to undergo an official assessment to attain my 12th Khan, officially certifying me as a Kru, a title endorsed by Grand Master Woody and other senior grand masters of KMA. The tour included rigorous daily training and ended with a formal evaluation by a panel of KMA grand masters, where I demonstrated Muay Thai and Muay Boran techniques as well as my teaching abilities. This trip also included intense Muay Boran and Krabi-Krabong workshops, as well as immersive sessions at Muay Thai sports gyms, where we trained twice daily. I was deeply honored when Senior Grand Master Phosawat Sangsawang, also known as Kru Pho, anointed me as a Kru. Even as an elder, Kru Pho moved with the grace of a young master, with immense wisdom and skill in Muay Boran and Sports Muay Thai. He reminded me that a true Kru leads by example, embodying integrity and wisdom both in training and in life.

Back in London, my classes continued to flourish. My sessions in Liverpool Street became known for their technical rigor, intensity, and vibrant atmosphere. Drawing from all my teachers—Arjan V's disciplined military-style training, Ralph Beale's dedication and skill, the positive intensity from my All Stars coaches, the invigorating sessions at Cobra Gym, and the playful expertise and practical knowledge of the grand masters in Thailand—I eventually developed my own teaching style emphasizing practical combat, fitness, personal growth, and a deep respect for Thai martial arts and culture.

Teaching became a way for me to help others transform, and I saw my students grow as they pushed themselves in each class. As my students progressed, some even entered organized fights—starting with nondecision interclub bouts and going up to amateur and professional fights. I supported each of them in their journeys.

Beyond the gym, my role as a teacher extended to helping young people defend themselves and build inner strength. Many teens who came to me had experienced bullying; I focused not only on physical defense techniques for them but also on self-control, de-escalation, and awareness, empowering them to think clearly under pressure and stand strong. I also trained women in Muay Thai and self-defense, providing them with the confidence and skills to feel secure. I've worked with corporate clients as well, helping them build fitness and mental resilience. Seeing students grow from uncoordinated beginners into capable martial artists was incredibly fulfilling.

Despite my satisfaction in teaching, I began to feel the strain of focusing entirely on others. My own lifelong passion for Muay Thai felt diluted, and as I aged, I noticed my fitness waning. While I still felt sharp during sparring, I was far from the peak fitness I once enjoyed. Years of discipline had kept me strong, but now I was going through the motions, caught in the routine of teaching.

My body had changed, and my diet had fluctuated over the years, from strict vegetarianism to a more flexible diet. My sweet tooth hadn't helped, and while I'd always kept my weight under control with training, age was catching up with me. I realized that I needed a change, not only in my diet and exercise, but in my outlook.

I needed a renewed approach to training, one that aligned with my evolving life. This wasn't just about physical fitness but about staying committed to growth even as my role shifted. I saw the importance of remaining a student of the art, dedicated to life-long learning and improvement, not only for my students' benefit but for my own well-being and passion for my martial journey.

TRADITIONS OF MENTAL STRENGTH AND SPIRITUAL POWER

While Muay Thai lacks a formalized spiritual doctrine, it embodies a profound philosophy grounded in personal growth, resilience, and spiritual awareness. Although not explicitly religious, Muay Thai aligns closely with the principles of Thai Buddhism and traditional Thai beliefs, instilling core values such as humility, respect, dedication, discipline, resilience, and mindfulness. This unspoken foundation shapes Muay Thai as not only a martial art but also a path of self-improvement and inner strength. Each training session is more than mere physical exercise; it's an opportunity for practitioners to cultivate new levels of awareness, self-discipline, and clarity.

Central to Muay Thai's philosophy is the concept of the warrior spirit, which transcends physical strength alone. This spirit requires fighters to face adversity with courage, maintain composure under pressure, and cultivate unbreakable determination. As they endure the demands of training and competition, fighters should seek mental resilience, learning to push beyond limitations.

The symbolism of Muay Thai draws on powerful animal and deity archetypes representing qualities like strength, agility, skill, and endurance. This also extends to a deeper connection with the natural elements of earth, fire, water, and air. Many fighters believe they can channel the essence of these elements, animals, and deities to connect themselves to a greater universal force.

For those pursuing a deeper spiritual journey, Muay Thai offers paths to mindfulness through both moving and still meditation. The rhythm and repetition of training cultivate a focused, meditative state, helping fighters stay present, clear-minded, and deeply attuned to their bodies and surroundings. In this way, Muay Thai becomes more than a sport, but rather a holistic journey linking practitioners to the larger spiritual forces that shape their lives. Through its blend of physical mastery, mental discipline, and spiritual practice, Muay Thai can be a powerful path to self-discovery and personal transformation.

WARRIOR'S SPIRIT: AN UNSTOPPABLE FORCE

A core philosophy of the warrior spirit is the idea of an unbreakable will—a fighter who, through the intense struggle of hard training and the challenges of battle, digs deep to rise victorious. The concept of training hard to fight with ease and the ethos of never giving up are embedded in the sport's history. This warrior spirit encapsulates essential qualities such as resilience, willpower, discipline, endurance, mental strength, honor, and respect that are not only crucial in combat but empower practitioners to be more capable people in everyday life. In Muay Thai, it's not just about the physical act of fighting; it's about developing a mental fortitude deeply enriched by spiritual and philosophical awareness.

The many esoteric and culturally rich rituals of Muay Thai are powerful expressions of the warrior spirit. Rituals honoring the spiritual world and invoking protection and strength from higher powers remind fighters that they are part of something greater than just a fighting sport and carry the legacy of their ancestors, their teachers, and their training camps. By performing these rituals, fighters bring respect not only to the gods and spirits that guide them but also to their craft, reinforcing the deeper spiritual dimensions of Muay Thai. These traditions reflect the resilience that defines a true fighter.

Key Components of a Warrior Spirit

While everyone is born with a warrior spirit, it may be dormant in some, awaiting activation through personal experiences or focused effort, while others find it naturally awakened. In Muay Thai training, students are encouraged to unlock this inner strength through disciplined and strategic practice under the guidance of skilled teachers. With consistent effort and dedication, anyone can activate their inner warrior.

The cultivation of a warrior spirit requires individuals to break through both internal and external barriers, delving into themselves to uncover their core strength and tenacity. This spirit is tempered by enduring suffering and defeat, ultimately emerging stronger and rising above adversity. The key components that define the psychological principles of the warrior spirit are:

> **Resilience.** This is the ability to withstand and overcome
> physical pain, mental challenges, and setbacks in both
> training and competition. Fighters are constantly tested
> by their opponents and their own limits, but the warrior

spirit embodies the idea of never giving up, bouncing back from injuries or defeats, and continuing to grow stronger with each challenge faced.

Willpower. In Muay Thai this is the inner drive that keeps fighters moving forward even when exhaustion, doubt, or fear creeps in. It is the mental strength that pushes fighters to dig deep and find the energy to continue through the toughest rounds of a fight or the most grueling training sessions. The warrior spirit thrives on the ability to maintain focus and determination no matter how difficult the journey becomes.

Discipline. This is central to Muay Thai for self-control and the dedication necessary to train rigorously, follow strict routines, and maintain focus over time. The warrior spirit ensures that fighters maintain discipline not just in physical training but in their mental approach and respect for the sport, their trainers, and themselves. Discipline fosters consistent progress and mastery of technique.

Endurance. In Muay Thai endurance is both physical and mental. Fighters must tolerate long training hours and the physical toll of repeated strikes, while fostering the stamina required to outlast an opponent in the ring. The warrior spirit emphasizes the need for perseverance and the ability to push through fatigue and discomfort, understanding that true growth happens beyond one's comfort zone.

Mental strength. Muay Thai is about focus, composure, and psychological resilience. A fighter must know how to create inner peace in the face of adversity. The warrior spirit enables fighters to maintain clarity and control even when under pressure or in the heat of battle. They must remain focused under intense pressure, maintain discipline, and keep a clear mind even when physically exhausted or up against a mighty challenge.

Honor. The way fighters conduct themselves inside and outside the ring reflects their honor. It's about upholding the values of the sport, showing integrity, and fighting with dignity. The warrior spirit is not just about victory, but about representing oneself, one's teacher, and one's camp honorably, as well as showing respect to opponents and the traditions of Muay Thai.

Respect. This is a key aspect of the warrior spirit. Fighters show respect to their teachers (Kru), their opponents, their gym, and the sport itself through rituals such as the Wai Khru and the Ram Muay to honor the lineage of Muay Thai and the people who have passed down its teachings.

A Nak Muay's Connection to the Natural World

Grand Master Woody taught me the path of a Nak Muay is deeply intertwined with nature, reflecting an ancient understanding of the interconnectedness of all life. This link with nature is not merely symbolic but actively cultivated through training environments and various practices and rituals.

Many Muay Thai and Muay Boran training camps in Thailand are in natural settings, such as outdoor camps. This allows practitioners to draw in fresh air and be energized by the sun, air, earth, and water. These beautiful environments include forests, mountains, grasslands, riversides, and by the ocean, each offering a tranquil backdrop that contrasts with the intensity of training. The natural surroundings help fighters find the inner peace and balance essential for their mental, emotional, and spiritual well-being.

The rhythm in nature gives fighters a means to attune themselves to the organic cadence and flow of real-life experiences. The rising and setting of the sun, the sounds of wildlife, and the changing weather patterns all contribute to a deeper awareness and mindfulness. All-weather training—whether on rainy days, hot sunny days, or other types of conditions—can help practitioners build resilience and understanding of life's ever-changing situations.

In these natural settings, practices such as walking, running, stretching, and mindfulness exercises can each connect a fighter to the integrated flow of life. These help fighters develop a calm and focused mind, essential for both combat and daily life.

Training barefoot in Muay Thai and Muay Boran is not just out of tradition; it's a profoundly impactful approach to connect fighters to the earth, enhancing their physical, mental, and spiritual well-being. Practitioners can thus engage their feet more naturally, which is crucial for optimizing the functionality of muscles, tendons, and ligaments. Such engagement improves the balance and stability essential for executing effective strikes and defensive maneuvers. Going shoeless means the muscles in the feet and lower legs work harder, which not only increases strength and endurance but also fosters a deeper sense of grounding. This connection to the earth isn't merely physical; it extends to mental health benefits as well. Being grounded physically can enhance stability and mindfulness, sharpen focus and confidence, and generally have a soothing effect on the nervous system, thereby reducing stress levels and boosting overall well-being.

Training without shoes has so many benefits; it is one of the unspoken cornerstones of martial arts disciplines like Muay Thai and Muay Boran.

Acknowledging the Elements: A Warrior's Awareness

Grand Master Woody taught me that everything in the world carries energy, and we are intrinsically connected to this universal force. According to him, understanding and embracing the essential elements of earth, water, fire, air, and metal are crucial for martial artists. These elements represent the fundamental energies of life, and for a martial artist, it is vital to harness and embody this awareness, aligning both the physical and spiritual self with the world's natural flow. This understanding is key to mastering not only the techniques but the deeper philosophy of Muay Thai.

For example, at a fundamental level, earth represents grounding; fire symbolizes energy; air embodies clarity; water signifies flow; and metal suggests hardness. However, each element extends beyond these basic associations to serve a multitude of physical, mental, and spiritual understandings.

For a Muay Thai practitioner or any martial artist, each element represents a unique philosophy and characteristic essential for achieving higher levels of martial mastery:

> **Earth** is the foundation of the physical realm, symbolizing stability and grounding. Earth is not merely a physical tool but a spiritual anchor, providing an unshakable base for strength and resilience to emanate from. Just as mountains stand tall and immovable, the warrior channels earth to remain steadfast, delivering blows that are not just powerful but deeply rooted in the essence of being.
>
> **Fire** is the essence of transformation, passion, and willpower. It represents the eternal flame within the soul, transcending limitations and igniting change. The fiery

energy burns away doubts and fears, leaving behind only the purity of purpose. Each strike infused with fire is not just an act of aggression but a manifestation of the warrior's dedication and determination.

Air signifies the breath of life, the subtle yet vital force that connects all beings. It represents wisdom, speed, and clarity. The element of air cultivates a strategic mind as swift and expansive as the wind. This element teaches the warrior to move with grace and precision, embodying freedom and transcending the physical limitations of combat to engage with heightened awareness.

Water is the symbol of life, renewal, and emotional depth. It embodies the principles of flow, fluidity, and adaptability. Just as water can carve through solid rock over time, with water a warrior can learn to move with persistence and fluidity, turning obstacles into opportunities. Water also represents the healing force within, offering the martial artist a source of inner rejuvenation and calm amid the chaos of battle.

Metal represents the qualities of inner strength, sharpness, and resilience. Metal is more than just armor; it is a reflection of an unbreakable spirit both physically and mentally. Like a finely honed blade, the warrior's resolve is sharp and unwavering, capable of cutting through adversity with clarity and purpose. Metal empowers a martial artist to embrace the storm, using discipline and true inner strength to withstand trials without losing integrity.

In this reflective interpretation, each element not only enhances the warrior's physical prowess but also deepens their spiritual journey, guiding them toward mastery of both the external and internal realms. The natural cycles of growth, decay, and renewal mirror the fighter's journey of continuous self-improvement and perseverance.

Through this deep bond with nature, Muay Thai or Muay Boran practitioners not only become better martial artists but also more balanced and harmonious individuals.

MINDFULNESS AND MEDITATION

For a Muay Thai practitioner, mindfulness is the art of cultivating focused awareness in the present moment, engaging both mind and body with purpose. It is maintaining a constant presence throughout all aspects of training, from mastering techniques to building endurance, flexibility, and mental resilience. Mindfulness in Muay Thai means being fully attuned to every movement, breath, and decision, whether during solo drills, pad work, or in the intensity of sparring, without distraction or judgment. This heightened awareness enables fighters to make precise decisions, maintain composure under pressure, and respond to challenges with clarity, strengthening not only their physical skills but also their mental resilience and personal growth.

Rituals like the Ram Muay and Wai Khru are powerful forms of moving meditation and mindfulness. Through these practices, fighters cultivate heightened awareness and connect with a deep sense of purpose through the honoring of their lineage, teachers, and heritage. This moving meditation fosters self-awareness, grounding fighters in their past, sharpening their vision for the future, and centring their focus on the present. As a mental, physical, and spiritual preparation, these rituals align fighters with their inner strength, readying them to face any challenge with respect, resilience, and clarity.

This blend of meditation, mindfulness, and physical prowess ensures that practitioners are not just fighters but also carry a balanced approach to life, managing stress and emotions effectively. The diverse beliefs and practices woven into Thai martial arts make it more than just a physical exercise: it is a deeply spiritual discipline that aims to develop the individual holistically, promoting physical agility, mental sharpness, and spiritual growth to harmonize the body, mind, and spirit.

Some traditional schools of Thai martial arts encourage advanced meditation techniques for Muay Boran, Krabi-Krabong, and Muay Thai practitioners such as visualizing movements and combat scenarios and focusing on the flow of energy to fortify their mental resilience. This tradition extends to quieting the mind, concentrating one's thoughts on a positive outcome, and engaging in mindfulness through focused breathing and body awareness.

All of this reminds us that Muay Thai is not simply about physical mastery, but also about the cultivation of mind and spirit, forging a profound connection between the practitioner and their cultural heritage.

CHAPTER TWELVE

RIGHTEOUS RULERSHIP

A METAMORPHOSIS OF FIRE AND WATER

Noticing that I had lost something I had always taken for granted was a rude awakening for me. Throughout my life, I had battled physical imbalances, but prided myself on a naturally muscular physique and being physically fit and mentally determined. As I reached my late thirties, I struggled to find the motivation to exercise. This, combined with poor nutrition and a more sedentary lifestyle, began to take a toll on my body. It felt like I was on a slippery slope, gradually losing the progress I'd worked so hard to achieve over the years. Fitness, strength, balance, and good health, once abundant, were now falling away. Years of martial arts training had instilled me with discipline and skill, but I had grown complacent and lost my focus. I had reached a plateau where my skills and fitness had become a standard, so I assumed they would remain intact without continued effort. It was a humbling realization that I needed to actively adapt and keep working if I wanted to maintain and progress in my abilities. With this newfound awareness, I sought out new avenues to enhance my physical skills and reignite my passion for learning.

My journey took an unexpected turn into a new realm of physical expression that complemented my martial arts abilities and opened me up to a whole new world of mastery. I took up the partnered dances of salsa and bachata, embracing them as liberating forms. Instead of the familiar routine of hard training, sparring, and exercising primarily with sweaty men, I found myself surrounded by sweet-smelling women on the dance floor. This move wasn't about seeking physical indulgence but new growth and awareness by a different means. Living a celibate life at the time, I wasn't using dance to meet women. Instead, through dance I gained more emotional clarity, spiritual awareness, social connection, and a new source of physical movement. It embodied a beautiful balancing of male and female energy, a unification of opposites, like the reunion of yin and yang.

At first, it was a challenge because, as the man, I needed to lead the dance routines. But as in life, how can you really lead if you don't know your role or what to do? This spoke volumes to me. I went from being advanced in martial arts to a complete novice in dance—an eye-opening experience. So I embraced the beginner's mind so valued in Buddhism and dedicated myself to weekly practice, pushing myself to learn and grow in this newfound passion. Over time, I did learn to lead various partners respectfully through complex dance routines. This experience deepened my understanding of nonverbal communication and the power of rhythm, timing, and flow.

As I progressed, my ability to shift my weight smoothly from one foot to another, coupled with an enhanced awareness of body language and flow, had a profound impact on my martial arts skills. I then discovered that many great fighters of the past had also used dance to enhance their movement. Bruce Lee, for example, studied cha-cha and credited it with improving his agility. Muhammad Ali, who was known for his incredible footwork, famously incorporated techniques inspired by his training in tap. Vasyl Lomachenko learned traditional Ukrainian dance before he even started boxing, which helped him develop his evasive movements. Saechai, regarded as one of the most skillful Thai fighters of all time, is known for his elusive footwork, unorthodox angles, and playful movement inside the ring; in fact, he is often seen dancing during training and warmups, using rhythm to enhance his agility. These legends recognized the value of dance for their agility, balance, and overall movement and had integrated it into their martial prowess.

My body and mind felt more balanced and capable than ever before. I had always exuded strong masculine energy, and years of rigorous warrior training had amplified that, however, dance allowed me to connect with my feminine energy. Balancing my energy had a significant impact on my self-healing journey. As a boy and moving into manhood, I had learned to walk through life with my guard up, like a warrior clad in heavy armor. But now, as an experienced warrior, I learned to connect more deeply with my heart and not always be on guard. I sought to walk as a peaceful guardian dressed in soft cotton, knowing I could bring out my warrior's nature when needed. As a result, I met my wife, and together we created a new life that led to the birth of our two beautiful, smart, and caring daughters. As they say, "All things in their time."

My physical injuries as a child had unconsciously contributed to many of the challenges that shaped the course of my life. Facing them had led me on a profound hero's quest of healing, understanding, and self-actualization. As a consequence of my dedicated self-healing journey, while not 100 percent healed, I now also felt more mentally, emotionally, and spiritually whole than ever before.

EARTHLY GOVERNANCE
AND SPIRITUAL GUIDANCE

The period following the fall of Ayutthaya in 1767 was one of the most tumultuous in Thai history. The once-glorious kingdom was left in ruins, heralding a dark time of disarray and fragmentation. Leadership voids and the chaos of warlord rivalries tore at the fabric of the Siamese nation until General Taksin emerged as a pivotal figure. His efforts to reunite the land under the newly established Thonburi Kingdom marked the first steps toward recovery. Yet, it was Thong Duang, a skilled military officer, who would rise through the ranks and, after King Taksin's fall from power, establish the enduring Chakri dynasty in 1782.

His reign signaled a profound shift that extended beyond mere political consolidation. In adopting the name "Rama I," referencing the Ramakien epic, he linked himself to Phra Narai, suggesting the moral and ethical leadership of this reincarnating deity. This title conveyed the virtues of loyalty, bravery, righteousness, and adherence to the Dharma. As the first ruler of the Chakri dynasty, King Rama I not only unified the kingdom but also revitalized Thai culture and spiritual heritage, setting a precedent for the kings who would follow.

Rama I's reign can be seen as a master class in the art of nation-building. By relocating the capital to Bangkok and constructing the Grand Palace, he not only physically fortified his authority but also reestablished and reinforced the spiritual and cultural identity of Siam. Campaigns to secure and expand Siamese territory both shored up Siam's foundation and demonstrated a dedication to Thai martial arts.

Being a devoted Buddhist, Rama I sought to restore key temples in the country, showing his commitment to spiritual renewal and moral leadership. His reign exemplified the dual role of Thai kings blending spiritual and temporal powers and underscored the holistic approach to leadership in Thai culture, balancing governance with spiritual stewardship. His legacy of tradition and innovation laid the groundwork for the modern Thai state and ensured stability and cultural continuity through the Chakri dynasty.

THE THAI MONARCHY'S RELATIONSHIP TO BUDDHISM

Throughout Thailand's history there has been a symbiotic relationship between the Thai monarchy and spirituality, tracing back to the Sukhothai Kingdom. It was during this era that King Ramkhamhaeng championing Theravada Buddhism as the state religion. His reign is regarded as the spiritual awakening of a nation. By shaping the destiny of his people under the guiding principles of the Dharma, the ethical and moral doctrine of Buddhism, he deeply influenced Thailand's cultural and spiritual life.

Subsequent Thai monarchs, revered as Dharmarajas, have carried on the legacy of intertwining governance with the spiritual tenets of Buddhism, embodying both moral and spiritual leadership. According to Thai Buddhist teachings, this title refers to a political and spiritual ruler who upholds and embodies the principles of the Dharma, cosmic law, and moral order. Thai monarchs even go so far as to take temporary ordination as Buddhist monks, reflecting a deep commitment to the spiritual well-being of their subjects.

The longest-reigning Thai monarch, King Bhumibol Adulyadej, also known as Rama IX, honored this tradition with his ordination following his grandmother's death in 1956. During his fifteen-day tenure as a monk, Rama IX wholeheartedly adopted a life of discipline and contemplation. An essential aspect of his monastic routine was participating in the traditional alms round when monks walk among the community at dawn collecting food offerings in their alms bowls, which typically constituted their main meal of the day. For the king, this was more than a daily routine; it was a profound exercise in humility and connection with the people. Adhering to the Buddhist tenet of moderation, his meals were limited to what was received during alms and consumed before noon.

The king devoted significant time to meditative practices and the study of Buddhist scriptures, deepening his grasp of the Dharma and mindfulness. He also partook in daily monastic responsibilities, embracing the values of service and community life. During his brief time in the monkhood, Rama IX was profoundly influenced by a sense of discipline, empathy, and a strong connection to Thailand's spiritual traditions, and these qualities impacted his reign. He was a compassionate and highly respected monarch deeply attuned to the ethos of his kingdom. Nationally, this reinforced the symbiotic relationship with Buddhism, highlighting the king's role in understanding and addressing the spiritual needs of his people. The Thai monarch works in partnership with the Supreme Patriarch, the head of Thai Buddhism, for a harmonious blend of royal authority and spiritual leadership.

As a Dharmaraja, the Thai monarch is entrusted to uphold the key spiritual elements of Buddhism, weaving them into the very fabric of governance and societal leadership. The king is considered a guardian of the Dharma, ensuring justice, moral integrity, and compassion guide his actions. he preserves temples, supports religious education, and promotes Buddhist teachings both domestically and internationally. Beyond governance, the king acts as a spiritual role model for the people, modeling mindfulness and detachment. Through active participation in Buddhist ceremonies and rituals, the monarch bridges Thailand's rich Buddhist heritage with modern society, reinforcing cultural continuity and spiritual identity. While this description paints the king as the good protector and benefactor of his people, not all Thai kings have fully lived up to this ideal. As in many cultures, absolute power can corrupt absolutely. The temptations of power and wealth can be too much for any human being. However, the lofty vision of divine rulership aims for a monarch to be more than just a ruler; they are expected to actively serve their people, using their position not for personal gain but to create a legacy that enhances the lives of their subjects. This view of leadership stresses the king's duty as a beneficial driver of the nation's welfare.

This concept of righteous leadership can extend beyond royals and serve as a guiding principle for leaders in business, social organizations, and even within families. Just like a monarch, leaders in all areas of society are entrusted with both power and responsibility and have the potential to significantly influence the lives of those they lead. By adopting a mindset of service, focusing on the well-being and development of their teams, communities, or families, leaders can create lasting positive impacts on the greater good and strive to leave a legacy of positive change.

The Chakri Dynasty: A Living Legacy

Since its inception in 1782, the Chakri dynasty has seen ten monarchs on the throne of Thailand. Each has left a lasting imprint on the country, shaping its political landscape, cultural heritage, and societal norms.

King Rama I (Phra Phutthayotfa Chulalok; r. 1782–1809) founded the Chakri dynasty and established Bangkok as Thailand's capital in 1782. His reign was characterized by significant reforms, including the restructuring and adaptation of the Ramakien. He compiled Thailand's first law code and was instrumental in reorganizing the Thai administration system, laying the groundwork for modern governance.

King Rama II (Phra Phutthaloetla Naphalai; r. 1809–1824) was known for his patronage of the arts and literature, which led to a renaissance in Thai poetry and culture.

King Rama III (Phra Nangklao; r. 1824–1851) reformed the tax and treasury system, expanded trade with China and the West and was involved in major temple constructions, which helped promote Buddhism.

King Rama IV (King Mongkut, Phra Chom Klao; r. 1851–1868) modernized Thailand through science and technology and secured the country's sovereignty during the colonial era. He was known in the West as the king in *Anna and the King of Siam*. Yet he was nothing like his portrayal in this book and the subsequent films; he was highly educated and sophisticated as a man and ruler.

King Rama V (King Chulalongkorn; r. 1868–1910) continued the modernization policies of his father, abolished slavery, and implemented numerous administrative and social reforms that drastically transformed Thai society.

King Rama VI (King Vajiravudh; r. 1910–1925) was known for promoting nationalism. He modernized the military and established the Thai educational system and was also a playwright and poet.

King Rama VII (King Prajadhipok; r. 1925–1935) was educated at Eton, and he was the last absolute monarch of Siam, becoming its first constitutional monarch after the Siamese revolution of 1932.

King Rama VIII (King Ananda Mahidol; r. 1935–1946) was only nine years old when he was chosen to be king succeeding Prajadhipok. His short reign ended in mysterious circumstances in 1946 when he was shot dead in his bedroom.

King Rama IX (King Bhumibol Adulyadej; r. 1946–2016) was the longest-reigning monarch in Thai history and one of the longest in world history. He ruled for seventy years and was deeply loved for his dedication to improving the lives of his people through numerous royal projects.

King Rama X (King Maha Vajiralongkorn) ascended the throne in 2016, following the death of his father King Bhumibol, and is the current king of Thailand.

The Chakri dynasty has continuously ruled Thailand since 1782, making 2025 the 243rd year of its reign—akin to Japan's Imperial House, which is the world's longest-serving dynasty at approximately 1,500 years. Similarly, the British royal family traces its origins back over one thousand years to Anglo-Saxon rulers before William the Conqueror's 1066 invasion, evolving through multiple dynasties—including the Plantagenets, Tudors, Stuarts, and Hanoverians—before the House of Saxe-Coburg and Gotha was renamed the House of Winsor in 1917. This enduring lineage places the Chakri dynasty among some of the world's longest-reigning royal families.

The Path of a Monk:
Walking the Middle Way

In Thailand, Buddhist monks are highly respected as protectors of the Dharma. They are revered not just as spiritual leaders but as integral pillars of society, embodying the teachings of the Buddha in every aspect of their lives. The profound interconnection between Buddhism and the state is reflected in the mutual relationship between the monarchy and the monastic community, underscoring their mutual significance in Thai culture.

Thai monks typically reside in monasteries known as *wats*. These sacred spaces are where monks embrace a life of simplicity, owning little more than their robes, an alms bowl, a needle, a water strainer, and a razor, in adherence to the strict Vinaya code of conduct. Each monk has all of their hair shaved off, including their eyebrows, to represent a shedding of worldly identity and attachments and a new beginning in the spiritual life.

A day in the life of a Thai monk is a journey through spiritual disciplines that shape both their character and their contribution to society. Their mornings begin before dawn, with morning chants and meditation, setting a tone of mindfulness and spiritual purity for the day ahead. This early start is followed by the traditional alms round, a poignant practice where monks walk through the community barefoot, collecting food offerings for them to eat. This ritual fosters a deep connection between monks and laypeople, emphasizing humility and the cyclical nature of giving and receiving. Afternoons are dedicated to personal study and meditation to deepen their spiritual understanding, alongside fulfilling monastery duties. They usually eat only once or twice in the morning and abstain from solid food after noon, though this is not strictly required by the Vinaya code, however, it does promote discipline and control over physical desires. Their diet is mainly vegetarian. They live a life of celibacy, restraint, and detachment from physical comforts and material possessions. They are expected to embody humility and compassion, showing kindness to all living beings and detaching from ego and personal desire.

Their existence is marked by a profound commitment to spiritual growth, humility, and compassion. They strive to embody these virtues, serving as moral guardians and spiritual mentors to the community, illustrating the profound impact of living a life dedicated to spiritual and societal service.

Senior monks often hold a special place in Thai society as wise sages and spiritual guides. Their deep understanding of Buddhist teachings enables them to offer solace and advice on moral and ethical dilemmas faced by their followers. They preside over religious ceremonies from the ordination of new monks to the blessing of new homes and businesses, embedding themselves deeply in the fabric of everyday life.

Through their disciplined lives and service, Thai monks promote a path of balance between extreme self-discipline and worldly indulgence. Thus, the path of a monk is a vivid illustration of the Buddha's Middle Way, offering a model of living that balances spiritual devotion with active community engagement. Their existence is a continual reminder of the possibility of enlightenment and the profound impact of living a life dedicated to spiritual and moral principles. This role not only sustains their personal spiritual journey but also enriches the collective spiritual health of Thai society.

Within Thai martial arts, monks provide warriors with spiritual support, helping them cultivate mindfulness, discipline, and resilience for both training and combat. Through rituals, blessings, sacred tattoos, and prayers, monks instill a sense of heritage, protection, guidance, respect, and remembrance.

These practices enable fighters to face challenges with mental peace, clarity, and determination while honoring their teachers, ancestors, and spiritual guardians—values upheld by the monks.

Monks act as moral compasses within Thai society, encouraging individuals, including Muay Thai practitioners, to live virtuous lives. By following Buddhist precepts such as nonviolence, honesty, and self-discipline, fighters are guided to approach their craft with honor and integrity. This moral framework fosters a culture of respect within the Muay Thai community, emphasizing that martial arts are not merely about physical combat but also about personal and spiritual growth.

Wats often serve as centers of community life, providing education, food, and guidance to local populations. Many Muay Thai fighters, coming from humble backgrounds, rely on these community networks for stability and encouragement. The monks' teachings deeply influence the environment in which practitioners are raised and trained, shaping their values and outlook.

By preserving traditions and fostering community well-being, Thai monks ensure that the essence of Thai culture remains vibrant and enduring. Their spiritual influence is seamlessly woven into the legacy of Muay Thai, enriching it with a depth that transcends the physical aspects of the martial art and embedding it firmly within the broader fabric of the nation.

CHAPTER THIRTEEN

MYTHOLOGY IN MARTIAL FORMS

NEW VISION AND ACTION LEADS TO CHANGE

As I transitioned into the life of a family man, the world went into the global lockdown of the coronavirus pandemic. This gave me more time with my family but less time for personal training and teaching my students in person, so I adapted by finding new ways to teach online. When the lockdown ended, new challenges awaited: the gym where I had taught for fifteen years had to close down. As a new father, I chose not to find a new venue immediately and decided to dedicate more time to my family. This decision was highly fulfilling, but after two years without my regular classes and only really training myself in part alongside my one-on-one clients, my fitness and overall well-being began to deteriorate again. The relentless march of time was an endless beating drum. Although I was still fitter than the average man who had never trained, I felt the effects of aging in my body. I needed to adapt again and find new ways to develop my body for this time of life.

I had journeyed through the stages of martial arts, evolving from novice to student, fighter to warrior, and coach to teacher, striving upward toward mastery. Life's journey, much like a spiral, involves continuous rotation, moving either upward or downward. We transition from newbie to apprentice, coach to teacher, master to ambassador, and then back to beginner as we learn new things. At this stage, I found myself returning to the role of a student. My focus shifted to mastering my body, emotions, mind, and spirit during the middle years of my life.

When I was younger, I explosively battled to discover the boundaries of my potential and cultivated deeper self-awareness, discipline, and skill. Now in my middle-aged years, I realized it was about refining my freedom of movement, cultivating more energy, and honing strategic effectiveness. I found that if I wanted to maintain or even climb higher on the ladder of martial mastery, I had to keep moving. I could not become idle and take my skills and abilities for granted, as they could easily be lost with time. I needed new methods for developing inner strength and resilience to balance the ever-increasing demands of life as I juggled family, work, and my own creative and introspective pursuits. This new awareness gave me the determination to prepare myself for future stages of life.

I have seen elders, both practitioners and teachers, who have only focused on the hard aspects of their training, and as they aged, their bodies broke from the strain. I've seen others who stopped training altogether, and their bodies either became weak with time or fat from excess. I then looked to others who had adapted as they aged, reaching new levels of self-mastery by balancing self-care with continued growth and development, reaching beyond merely physical progression and ascending to higher states of enlightenment.

I now look ahead with a clear vision and a long-term goal of living a healthy life enriched by martial wisdom and practice. My aim is to keep developing and progressing, continuing my

Muay training with a focus on deepening my understanding. While I may not be driven to push myself in hard sparring in the way I once did, I plan to maintain my strength and fitness through adaptive workouts, honing the flow of my technical abilities.

I recognize the importance of deepening my connection to my breath and aligning with the natural world, striving to create a balance between the rooted hard and pliable soft training like night complements day. I embrace the knowledge, wisdom, and tactical skills I've gained, and I remain open to learning from all experiences.

As I now lived too far from Arjan V for regular training, with his blessing, I sought coaches closer to home to break out of my idleness. I became a new student again, learning different styles of teaching and training in Muay Thai, tai chi, and qigong.

This new rotation in my martial journey positioned me as a masterful student, humble in the learning process and diligent in acquiring new skills as I aged. The passage through the stages of life presents us with unexpected twists and turns that require us to adjust and grow. It's essential that we learn to adapt in order to lead fulfilling and meaningful lives.

Ultimately, I understand that each phase of the martial arts journey teaches us that true mastery is not in defeating others, but in understanding and transcending ourselves. This renewed dedication is about adapting to the changes within, embracing the lessons that come with age, and seeking new avenues of growth and self-mastery.

After nearly two years of dedicated practice, I restored my strength and fitness while deepening my understanding of training and martial arts. It now felt like the right time to reestablish my classes, but this time in Shepherd's Bush on the opposite side of London. This marked an exciting new chapter in my journey, as I set out to build my own martial arts school: LionHeart Muay Thai Academy.

MARTIAL INSPIRATION FROM
STORIES OF THE GODS

During my years of Muay training, I initially learned Muay Boran from Arjan V and later from renowned teachers like Grand Master Woody, General Amnat, Grand Master Sena, Master Ekger Mono, and others. I trained in a range of Boran techniques, beginning with the foundational form known as Mae Mai (Mother Techniques), referring to the fundamental or core techniques, and then into Luk Mai (Child Techniques), referring to the advanced or refined techniques that build on the basics. I also trained in specialized animal forms such as Hanuman, Tiger, and Elephant. These foundational styles are essential to mastering Muay Boran's principles and movements, which also subtly inform modern Muay Thai.

As discussed earlier, Muay Boran regional styles incorporate distinctive techniques inspired by Thai mythology, natural elements, and battlefield tactics. Each movement connects practitioners with Thai cultural heritage and the spiritual essence of figures from the Ramakien, animals, and revered deities.

An excellent example of Thai mythology in Muay Boran can be found in the sixteen Muay Lopburi Mae Mai techniques. This style is said to be the oldest Muay Boran tradition, established by the hermit sage Sukatanta of the Khao Samor Khon Martial Art School in Lopburi. It is characterized by fluid yet powerful techniques. Muay Lopburi integrates the movements of animals and mythic figures, creating a graceful yet lethal martial art.

THE SIXTEEN TECHNIQUES OF MUAY LOPBURI MAE MAI

ELEPHANT-INSPIRED TECHNIQUES

1. **Erawan Soei Nga (Elephant Tusk Uppercut)** counters an opponent's attack with an uppercut to the chin, mimicking the force of Erawan's tusks.
2. **Kotchasarn Torn Ya (Elephant Plucking Weeds)** neutralizes a kick by grabbing the opponent's ankle and throwing them off-balance.
3. **Kotchasarn Taeng Nga (Elephant Thrusting Tusks)** responds to a high kick by delivering a powerful double-elbow strike to the chest.
4. **Hak Nguang Aiyara (Breaking an Elephant's Trunk)** intercepts a body kick by catching the leg and countering with an elbow strike to the thigh.
5. **Hak Kor Erawan (Breaking Erawan's Neck)** counters a punch with a neck strike and a double-knee attack to the face.

MONKEY AND HANUMAN-INSPIRED TECHNIQUES

1. **Ling Ching Look Mai (Monkey Fighting for Fruits)** protects against a body kick by closing in on the opponent and delivering a double-fist strike to the chin.
2. **Ling Pliu (Flexible Monkey)** evades a high kick by ducking and countering with a knee to the opponent's back.

3. **Hanuman Torn Toh (Hanuman Removes a Stump)** counters a midlevel kick by grabbing the foot and delivering a kick to the pelvic area.

4. **Hanuman Tawai Waen (Hanuman Offering the Ring)** is a double-fist attack meant to disorient the opponent.

5. **Khunyak Jab Ling (A Giant Catching a Monkey)** intercepts a punch by locking the opponent's neck with an arm hold.

TECHNIQUES INSPIRED BY MYTHIC CHARACTERS

1. **Pha Ram Now Sorn (Rama Shooting an Arrow)** counters an elbow strike by catching the opponent's elbow and pushing it backward.

2. **Khun Yak Pha Nang (An Ogre Kidnapping a Lady)** counters a knee by positioning behind the opponent, pulling them down, and driving a knee into their back.

3. **Hiran Muan Phan Din (Ogre Hiran Rolling the Earth)** intercepts a body kick with an elbow to the thigh, followed by an elbow strike to the head.

4. **Yok Khao Phra Sumen (Lifting Mount Sumeru)** counters a straight punch with an uppercut to the chin, followed by rapid punches to the face.

5. **Guang Liao Lang (A Deer Looking Back)** dodges a punch by shifting right and countering with a kick to the torso.

6. **Lom Ploy Aye (When the Enemy Falls, You Feel Embarrassed Too)** instructs the practitioner to fall onto the opponent after they hit the ground and deliver an elbow strike to the chest or foot.

Each of these techniques, embodying mythological inspiration and natural symbolism, represents the intricate fusion of culture, combat, and philosophy in Muay Boran. Through these movements, practitioners not only hone their physical abilities but also connect to the spiritual and cultural heritage that defines Thai martial arts.

MASTER TECHNIQUES IN MUAY BORAN

The term *Mae Mai* often translates to major techniques, representing the core evasive and counterattacking movements in Muay Boran. Luk Mai is often regarded as minor techniques, but it more accurately refers to the child of the mother, or the evolution and next generation of skills and knowledge. Mae Mai represent the *fundamental* techniques essential for all practitioners to master. These moves form the base of essential balance, power, and positioning principles. Once a practitioner has developed a solid foundation of the Mae Mai form and application, they usually progress to Luk Mai techniques, which are more sophisticated and often more difficult to execute. The Mae Mai techniques are a gateway to subtler strategies, where practitioners refine their skills and embody the essence of traditional Thai combat. Luk Mai techniques complement the Mae Mai foundation with advanced maneuvers, traditionally reserved for students who have proven their skill and earned their teacher's trust. Both Mae Mai and Luk Mai have regional variations allowing each style to evolve with unique tactical adaptations.

Across Thailand, these master techniques have been carefully refined and codified by generations of Siamese warriors and masters, who distilled their combat wisdom into a system that upholds both the effectiveness and cultural heritage of Muay Boran. In the following section are fifteen Mae Mai master techniques taught to me on my training journey. They serve as a foundation of Muay Boran techniques and each move carries the strength and spirit of Thai cultural tradition.

THE FIFTEEN MAE MAI TECHNIQUES (MOTHER TECHNIQUES)

1. Salab Fan Pla (สลับฟันปลา—Crossing the Fishes Tail)

This technique involves a swift and deceptive movement to evade an opponent's attack, stepping outside their weapons and counterattacking. The cultural significance reflects Hanuman's swift agility and fluid movement to evade the sea creature's attack when he was crossing the ocean to rescue Sida.

How to implement: Used to dodge or block an opponent's straight punch by moving outside their weapons. It then opens up possibilities to control the attacker's arm setting up many different counterattacks.

2. Pak Sa Weak Rang (ปักษาแหวกรัง—Bird Breaks the Nest)

This involves stepping forcefully into the range of the opponent while they attack, breaking their guard or stance and setting up a disruptive counterattack. The imagery of a bird breaking through or disrupting a nest emphasizes how animal behavior has influenced Thai culture and martial arts.

How to implement: As the attacker throws a hook or straight punch, the defender swiftly steps into the attacker's guard, blocking their attack and counterattacking with an elbow to the face at the same time as their block.

3. Chawa Sat Hork (ชวาซัดหอก—Javanese Spear Thrust)

This technique involves ducking under an attacker's straight punch and countering with a forceful elbow strike. This mimics the thrusting motion of a magical spear like some of the weapons in Thai mythology. The term *Chawa* (Javanese) also hints at the historical interactions between Thai and Javanese cultures.

How to implement: As the attacker throws the straight punch, the defender ducks down low and moves outside the opponent's attack while counterattacking with a close-range strike—often an elbow to the attacker's solar plexus.

4. Inao Thang Grit (อิเหนาแทงกริช—Hanuman Presents the Ring)
This is another effective defense and counter against a straight punch by moving low and inside the attacker's range. This technique is directly inspired by the Ramakien and the character of Hanuman. It involves a graceful and precise movement to mimic Hanuman offering the ring to Sida as proof that he was sent by Pha Ram.

How to implement: As the attacker throws the straight punch, the defender steps diagonally toward the attacker and bends low. In this position, the defender moves inside the attacker's range to strike with a power elbow or punch to the chest.

5. Yok Khao Prasu Meru (ยกเขาพระสุเมรุ—Lifting Mount Sumeru)
This technique involves moving inside to slip or duck underneath an opponent's straight punch to open up a devastating counterattack. This symbolizes a fighter having the godly strength to lift the sacred mountain that is considered the center of the universe in Hindu and Buddhist cosmology. The act of lifting or moving something so monumental as Mount Sumeru reflects immense determination, a common theme within the Ramakien.

How to implement: As the attacker throws a straight punch, the defender slips or ducks under the opponent's straight punch, moving inside their guard to counterattack with a powerful punch under the chin that lifts them off the ground.

6. Ta Then Kam Fah (ตาเถรค้าฟ้า—Old Monk Holds the Melon)
This technique involves blocking and striking strategically at the same time. The image of an old monk holding up the wooden post that supports a large melon symbolizes balance, power, and mindful control, reflecting the harmony of a monk living in tune with the natural world.

How to implement: As the attacker throws a straight punch, the defender, at close range, raises their arm to block the strike while simultaneously delivering an uppercut to the opponent's chin.

7. Morn Yan Lak (มอญยันหลัก—Burmese Prop the Pillar)
This technique involves using a well-timed push kick (Teep) to counter an incoming attack, turning the opponent's momentum against them and knocking them backward. The term *Morn* is linked to the Mon people who have a significant presence in both Thailand and Burma. The phrase *Prop the Pillar* implies a stance or movement that embodies stability, support, or defense, much like propping up a pillar to stop it from falling.

How to implement: As the attacker rushes in with an attack, the defender counterattacks with both arms placed out in front to guard the face, while at the same time throwing a front foot push kick into the chest or abdomen of the attacker to force them away.

8. Pak Look Toy (ปักลูกทอย—Plunging the Stake)
This is a powerful defensive attack against a shin kick by throwing a counterattack with a double elbow strike into the attacker's shin and quad. This move evokes the act of driving a stake into the ground, suggesting a movement that involves a strong, decisive thrust aimed at immobilizing an opponent's leg and establishing a firm defensive position.

How to implement: As the attacker attempts to kick, the defender moves sideways, aligning with the attacker's kick, and uses their elbow to forcefully intercept it, targeting the attacker's shin or thigh. If using both arms, they could block and strike both areas simultaneously.

9. Jara Khe Fad Hang (จรเข้ฟาดหาง—Crocodile Swings Its Tail)
This technique is performed by throwing a deceptive initial punch or kick and appearing to lose one's balance, only to then swing back around with a powerful heel kick to the opponent's head. Inspired by the natural movement of a crocodile powerfully swinging its tail, it reflects the influence of animal behavior on Muay Boran techniques. In this context, the move is named after the powerful, sweeping motion a crocodile makes, with its tail used for propulsion in water or defensively to create space between itself and a threat.

How to implement: The defender swiftly jumps to the side, evading the attacker's punch, while throwing a purposely missed attack while shielding their face. They then twist their body back around to deliver a powerful heel kick aimed at the attacker's abdomen or head.

10. Hak Nguang Aiyara (หักงวงอัยรา—Breaking the Elephant's Trunk)
This involves a defensive maneuver to break or evade an opponent's powerful shin kick by catching the leg and throwing an elbow into the attacker's thigh or knee joint. This technique draws inspiration from how elephants were used in war as weapons and symbolizes breaking a mighty attack.

How to implement: As the attacker launches a kick toward the body, the defender quickly wraps an arm around the attacking leg, effectively catching it. Simultaneously, they lift their opposite arm high and then forcefully bring down their elbow onto the attacker's thigh or into the side of the knee joint.

11. Naga Bid Hang (นาคาบิดหาง—Serpent Twists Its Tail)

This technique defends against a push kick to the body, with the defender catching the foot and with both hands, twisting it, then launching a solid knee to the back of the leg. A naga is a mythical serpentlike creature with roots in Hinduism, Buddhism, and Jainism widely revered in Southeast Asian cultures. Just as Hanuman beat the serpentlike creatures in the Ramakien as he crossed the ocean, this counterattack involves agile and fluid movements to catch a serpent and defeat it with a purposely focused strike.

How to implement: When the attacker launches a push kick, the defender swiftly catches the foot, securing it with one hand on top and the other underneath, simultaneously twisting the foot outward to potentially harm the ankle and leg. Following this, they execute a strong knee strike to the attacker's leg.

12. Viroon Hok Glab (วิรฬฟหกกลับ—Reversing the Situation)

This neutralizes a shin kick by countering with a push kick aimed at the attacker's quad or hamstring, using the heel to intercept and impact the target area. Metaphorically this technique is about using wit, agility, and tactical thinking to flip from a disadvantageous position or moment into an advantageous one.

How to implement: The defender swiftly executes a push kick toward the attacker's quad and hamstring, while simultaneously using both arms to protect their face. This quick and powerful kick is aimed at making the attacker spin around and lose their balance.

13. Dab Chawala (ดับชวาลา—Extinguishing the Lamp)
This technique defends against a straight punch by countering with a direct punch to the opponent's eye or face. It is designed to quickly neutralize an opponent's ability to continue fighting, similar to how one would snuff out a flame. Drawing from natural elements it emphasizes using strategic maneuvers to disrupt the opponent's perception and balance, effectively ending their offensive capabilities.

How to implement: The defender quickly steps forward and to the inside, dodging the attacker's straight punch. They tap the punch downward and counter with a powerful overhand punch aimed at the attacker's eye or face, impairing their vision and concentration.

14. Khun Yak Chab Ling (ขุนยักษ์จับลิง—Giant Catches the Monkey)
This very important move can empower a defender when fighting against a quicker, more agile, and tricky opponent. The metaphor of a giant capturing a nimble monkey suggests a move that combines strength and precision to counteract an opponent's agility and speed. This move brings together multiple actions, defending punches, kicks, elbows, and knees.

How to implement: The attacker launches a straight punch, and the defender quickly raises their elbow in front of their face deflecting and blocking the punch. The attacker then launches a right shin kick toward the defender's body. The defender swiftly uses their elbows to block the kick, striking back at the attacker's thigh and shin. When the attacker aims a downward chopping elbow at the defender's head, the defender swiftly ducks down, raising their arm to block and deflect the elbow. As the attacker tries to knee the defender, the defender moves backward with a quick half-step and counters with their own downward chopping elbow into the attacker's thigh. The attacker then attempts a shin kick to the defender's leg, yet the defender blocks it with their shin. Then, when the attacker attempts a kick to the head, the defender ducks under it to avoid contact.

15. Hak Kor Erawan (หักคอเอราวัณ—Breaking the Neck of Erawan)

This swift and direct finishing move counters an attacker's straight punch. Erawan is the Thai name for Airavata, the three-headed mythical white elephant who serves as the mount for Indra, the king of the gods in Hindu mythology. In Thai culture, Erawan is often associated with power, strength, and protection. The technique's name suggests a decisive move aimed at a critical point of an opponent, much like targeting the neck, which is a vulnerable spot. The imagery of breaking the neck of such a powerful creature as Erawan implies that this move is meant to be a finishing technique used to subdue an opponent effectively and swiftly.

How to implement: When the attacker launches a straight punch toward the defender's head, the defender slips inside the punch, avoiding it. They then grab the back of the attacker's shoulder and neck, pulling the head down. Simultaneously, the defender jumps up to deliver a knee strike to the attacker's face.

CONCLUSION

Since I began my Muay Thai journey at sixteen, this art has guided me through physical challenges, personal growth, and spiritual discovery. Years of training have taught me that martial arts are about far more than self-defense, competition, or fighting others—in essence it's about mastering self.

When I reestablished my martial arts academy in West London, starting from humble beginnings, it reminded me of the importance of perseverance, adaptability, and staying grounded in past lessons. Teaching others has been both a privilege and a responsibility, as I strive to pass on not just techniques but also the values and insights that Muay Thai embodies.

As a martial artist, I have no desire for conflict, yet I am equipped to handle it. I am a peaceful warrior seeking to live life respectfully and honorably, continuing the traditions of the old adapted for the modern age. As a father, I now have the gift and duty of teaching my children martial arts. My two daughters stand on my shoulders, and I am dedicated to supporting their development. While I don't particularly want them to become fighters, I want to give them the tools to become whoever they choose to be. My primary goal is to protect them, but more importantly, to teach them how to protect themselves.

Teaching my daughters martial arts has deepened my understanding of its purpose. The world is full of dangers, both in nature and human society; it's crucial for everyone to be prepared rather than caught unaware. Beyond establishing their physical skills, I aim to instill in them discipline, self-confidence, awareness, and respect for others. The ability to navigate life's dangers, both physical and emotional, with wisdom and composure is invaluable. Martial arts teach us to protect ourselves and those around us and to act with integrity and respect the interconnectedness of all life.

Through martial arts, I aim to instill these values and skills in my daughters and students alike, empowering them to navigate the world with confidence and resilience. My journey as a teacher is now even more illuminated by the joys of guiding others along the path of self-mastery through martial arts. Starting my own academy has brought its own set of challenges. I was meeting new students and developing a new following almost from scratch. Some of my previous students returned to my new classes, but it was a long journey for most, as I was in a completely new location. It was a humbling experience to transition from having booming classes of thirty to forty students in each session to starting with between one and two students in each class during the early days. Despite the initial small numbers, I stood balanced and confident, grounded in years of experience both in practice and teaching. I had faith in the tried-and-tested martial arts system I had become an ambassador of, and I was ready once again to share the lessons and understanding I had gained.

Muay Thai is more than a martial art; it is a profound journey of self-discovery and transformation, deeply rooted in the traditions, spirituality, and history of Thailand. It is a path that empowers practitioners to transcend mere physical prowess, fostering mental resilience, ethical living, and holistic well-being.

From its origins as Muay Boran, a liberating fighting system that empowered the Siamese people to defend their way of life, Muay Thai has evolved into a modern combat sport while preserving its essence of honor, discipline, and spiritual connection.

This art form has stood the test of time, proving itself as both a highly effective fighting system and a living embodiment of Thailand's cultural and spiritual heritage. Muay Thai rituals, such as the Wai Khru, Ram Muay, and sacred ceremonies, reveal the deeper layers of this martial art. They connect practitioners to the wisdom of the past, honoring teachers, ancestors, and spiritual guardians. These traditions remind us that Muay Thai is not just about fighting; it is a way of life that builds character, instills values, and teaches resilience. By embracing the embedded principles of Muay Thai, practitioners cultivate balance, courage, mindfulness, and compassion, empowering themselves to face life's challenges with integrity and purpose.

The stories of Thai martial heroes and mythology inspire this journey. Figures like King Naresuan, who endured captivity and emerged stronger to lead his nation to victory, demonstrate resilience and strategic mastery. The Tiger King teaches us that great power must be balanced with discipline to prevent self-destruction. Nai Khanomtom, the legendary fighter who reclaimed his freedom through skill and determination, reminds us that perseverance can overcome even the direst circumstances. These stories embody the warrior spirit of Muay Thai. They echo the determination of willpower to face adversity with unyielding resolve and to never give up, no matter the odds.

Even in the Ramakien, we find timeless lessons of teamwork, sacrifice, and martial excellence. When the realms of righteousness were threatened, it was through unity, strategy, and unwavering faith that good triumphed over evil. These tales, interwoven with Thai culture and martial arts, illuminate the depth and wisdom that Muay Thai embodies as a practice and a way of life.

Just as the warriors of old used their skills to adapt to changing times, modern practitioners of Muay Thai can draw from its rich traditions to elevate themselves and inspire others. Beyond physical prowess, Muay Thai offers a path to becoming well-rounded individuals, embodying the values of respect, discipline, and compassion. By embracing the virtues of legendary figures like the monkey god Hanuman or Pha Ram, the royal incarnation of Vishnu, practitioners can transform not only themselves but also those around them into beacons of strength, wisdom, and kindness.

Muay Thai, at its heart, is a powerful martial art that encourages living with purpose, integrity, and resilience. It teaches us that true strength comes not just through defeating opponents; instead, it focuses on safeguarding ourselves and elevating others, valuing our heritage, and aiming for continuous self-improvement. As we carry forward this legacy, may we always remember to embody the warrior spirit, not only in the ring but in every aspect of our lives.

GLOSSARY

Angkor: Historical capital of the Khmer Empire.

Angkor Wat: The most famous temple complex of Angkor, originally built as a Hindu temple dedicated to Vishnu, later used for Buddhist worship.

Animism: A belief system where all elements of nature, including animals, plants, and even inanimate objects, are believed to have a spiritual essence and consciousness.

Arjan: The Thai term for "master teacher," used in Muay Thai, Buddhism, and traditional arts.

Asura Realm: One of the six realms of existence in Buddhist cosmology, inhabited by demigods often involved in conflicts.

Bangkok: Capital and largest city of Thailand, established as the capital in 1782 by King Rama I.

Brahma: In Thai Buddhism, Brahma is revered as Phra Phrom, a god of creation. He is often depicted in a more accessible, devotional form than his Hindu counterpart, embodying purity and moral order.

Bodhi tree: The tree under which Siddhartha Gautama attained enlightenment, becoming the Buddha.

Bodhisattva: A being who attains enlightenment but chooses to stay in samsara to help others, central to Mahayana Buddhism.

Boons: In Hinduism and Buddhism, boons are divine gifts or blessings granted by gods in response to the penance, devotion, or prayers of devotees. They often include supernatural abilities, immense strength, or other miraculous powers that can dramatically alter the recipient's life.

Brahma: In Hinduism, the god of creation; in Thai culture, known as Phra Phrom.

Brahma Realms: Highest realms in Buddhist cosmology, where beings experience the greatest pleasures and have long lifespans.

Buddha: Title for Siddhartha Gautama, founder of Buddhism, after his enlightenment.

Buddhism: Major world religion based on the teachings of Siddhartha Gautama, focusing on overcoming suffering through moral conduct, meditation, and insight.

Burmese Kingdom: Historical region in modern-day Myanmar, frequently in conflict with Thai kingdoms.

Chakravartin: In Hinduism, an ideal universal ruler who upholds Dharma across the world. In Buddhism, a righteous monarch governed by Dharma, also symbolically linked to the Buddha as a spiritual wheel-turner. In Jainism, one of twelve sovereigns per cosmic half-cycle, is said to possess nine treasures and rule six continents.

Chakri Dynasty: The ruling royal house of Thailand since 1782, started by King Rama I.

Chatulangkabat or Muay Lang: Elite royal guards skilled in Muay Boran, tasked with protecting the Thai king.

Deva Realms: Heavenly realms in Buddhist cosmology, characterized by great pleasure and conditions favorable to achieving enlightenment.

Devaraja: The "God King" concept in Southeast Asian Hindu-Buddhist monarchies, where rulers were seen as divine incarnations of a god, often Vishnu or Shiva.

Dharma/dharma: In Hinduism, it means duty and cosmic order. In Buddhism, it refers to the Buddha's teachings and the path to enlightenment.

Dharmaraja: A title used for Thai kings, implying rulership guided by Dharma, the cosmic law.

Erawan: Erawan is the Thai name for Airavata, the three-headed mythical white elephant who serves as the mount for Indra, the king of the gods in Hindu mythology.

Four Noble Truths: Central teachings of Buddhism that diagnose the nature of suffering and prescribe a treatment for it.

Grantha: An ancient Indian script primarily used in Tamil Nadu and Kerala for writing Sanskrit and some of the Dravidian languages. It dates back to at least the sixth century and was used extensively for inscribing sacred and secular texts.

Hinduism: A major world religion originating in the Indian subcontinent, encompassing a variety of beliefs and practices.

Jainism: An ancient Indian religion focused on nonviolence, karma, and asceticism, distinctly different from Hinduism and Buddhism.

Kard Chuek: Traditional Muay Thai hand wrappings made from hemp or cotton rope.

Khmer Empire: A powerful empire in Southeast Asia, lasting from the ninth to the fifteenth century, known for its sophisticated culture and monumental architecture like Angkor Wat.

King Bhumibol Adulyadej: The ninth king of Thailand from the Chakri dynasty, revered for his long and beneficial reign.

King Jayavarman II: Founder of the Khmer Empire in the ninth century, declared himself a god-king or devaraja. He declared independence from Java and established his capital in present-day Cambodia, initiating a period marked by vast architectural and cultural development.

King Rama I–X: Kings of the Chakri dynasty, with King Rama I founding Bangkok as the capital and subsequent kings continuing his legacy. Rama X, Vajiralongkorn, is the current reigning king of Thailand.

King Ram Khamhaeng: The third ruler of the Sukhothai Kingdom, Thailand, reigning from 1279 to 1298. Credited with creating the Thai alphabet and promoting Buddhism, his reign marked a golden age of prosperity and cultural development in Thai history.

Krabi-Krabong: A traditional Thai weapons-based martial art using swords, staves, spears, shields, and hand-to-hand combat. It was developed alongside Muay Boran.

Kru/Khru: Thai word for "teachers," used in education, Muay Thai, and traditional arts and showing a deep cultural respect for instructors.

Kshatriya caste: The warrior and ruler caste in the traditional Hindu caste system.

Kubera: The god of wealth and king of the yakshas in Hindu mythology, he is also the guardian of the treasures of the gods and a benefactor of riches to his devotees. He is often depicted as a plump man adorned with jewels and carrying a money pot or bag.

Luk Muay: The "Child" or minor techniques, which are the next stage of advanced studies after students have mastered the Mae Mai (Mother Techniques).

Lanka: In the Ramakien, the kingdom ruled by the Demon King Tosakan, analogous to Sri Lanka in the Indian epic Ramayana.

Mae Mai: The "Mother" or major techniques that form the foundation of Muay Boran, the ancient battlefield system that subtly influences the modern sport of Muay Thai.

Mahayana Buddhism: A major branch of Buddhism emphasizing compassion, the Bodhisattva path, and universal enlightenment.

Mani People: Indigenous group living in Thailand, known for their traditional seminomadic lifestyle.

Manusya Realm: The human realm in Buddhist cosmology, characterized by both suffering and the potential for enlightenment.

Meditation: A practice integral to Buddhism and Muay Thai training, involving deep mental concentration and mindfulness.

Middle Way: In Buddhism, the balanced approach to spiritual development is between the extremes of abstinence and indulgence.

Mongkon: A sacred headband worn by Muay Thai fighters, believed to bring good luck, protection, and spiritual blessings.

Mount Sumeru: The mythical and spiritual mountain that connects all realms of the universe, known as Mount Meru in Hinduism and Mount Sumeru in Buddhist cosmology.

Muay Boran: An ancient battlefield fighting system from Siam, modern-day Thailand, this is the precursor to the modern sport of Muay Thai.

Muay Thai: Traditional Thai martial art known as "The Art of Eight Limbs," utilizing punches, kicks, elbows, and knee strikes.

Naga/Nagini: Serpentine deities in Hindu-Buddhist mythology associated with giant snakes, water, protection, and spiritual power. Naga (male), nagini (female).

Nai Khanomtom: Legendary Muay Thai fighter known for his victory over Burmese fighters in the eighteenth century.

Nak Muay: A traditional Muay Thai fighter. Nak Muay Farang refers to foreign practitioners of Muay Thai.

Naraka Realm: The lowest realm in Buddhist cosmology similar to hell, where beings suffer for their negative karma.

Negrito: A term for various ethnic groups in Southeast Asia, characterized by their African features, dark brown skin, and small stature. They are thought to be among the region's earliest inhabitants.

Pali: An ancient language of the Indian subcontinent, widely used in the Theravada Buddhist scriptures and also the liturgical language of Theravada Buddhism.

Pannung: Traditional Thai garment, a type of loincloth worn by Muay Thai fighters in the past.

Phra/Pha: A Traditional Thai term to represent sacred figures and deities. It can mean "venerable" or "holy."

Phra In: The Thai term for Indra, the Hindu king of the gods, ruler of the Devas (heavenly beings), associated with thunder, war and rain. Often depicted riding Erawan (Airavata), a multi-headed elephant.

Phra Isuan: The Thai term for Shiva, the Hindu god of destruction and transformation. Revered in Thai and Khmer traditions and often seen in temples as a supreme deity.

Phra Lak: Brother and companion of Phra Ram in the Ramakien, analogous to Lakshmana in the Ramayana.

Phra Narai: The Thai term for Vishnu, the Hindu god of protection and preservation. In Thai culture he is often depicted with four arms, holding a divine weapon, and is associated with kingship and stability.

Phra Ram/Pha Ram: The reincarnation of Vishnu, the hero of the Ramakien, the Thai version of Rama from the Ramayana. Phra Ram is the human incarnation of Vishnu, and all kings with the title of Rama are linked to his incarnation on Earth, representing him as a preserver of the universe. He is often depicted as a king and a protector, embodying virtues and leadership qualities.

Pra Jiads: The sacred armbands worn by Muay Thai fighters believed to offer protection and good luck.

Preta Realm: A realm in Buddhist cosmology inhabited by spirits suffering from intense desires and unsatisfied cravings.

Luang Sorasak, The Tiger King (Somdet Pra Sanphet VIII): A legendary monarch known as the "Tiger King" in Thai history. Born Prince Ma Deua, he was later known as Somdet Pra Sanphet VIII. His reign is celebrated for its military prowess and contributions to Muay Thai.

Ramakien: The Thai national epic, derived from the Indian Ramayana, incorporating Thai legends, characters, and values.

Sak Yant: Traditional Thai tattoos with spiritual significance, often worn by fighters for protection.

Samsara: In Buddhism and Hinduism, the cycle of birth, death, and rebirth, from which followers seek liberation.

Sanskrit: An ancient language of India, in which the Hindu scriptures and classical Indian epic poems are written and from which many northern Indian languages are derived.

Shiva: Known as Phra Isuan in Thai, a major Hindu deity known as the destroyer and regenerator of the universe, associated with meditation and arts. He is recognized as a powerful deity associated with creation and destruction, often worshipped for his role as a cosmic dancer who controls the movement of the universe.

Siamese kingdoms: Refers to the historical regions and political entities in what is now Thailand. The most notable Siamese kingdoms included Sukhothai and Ayutthaya, each known for its significant contributions to the region's cultural, religious, and political landscapes.

Sida: Character in the Ramakien, analogous to Sita in the Ramayana, known for her beauty and virtue.

Siddhartha Gautama: Known as the Buddha, Siddhartha Gautama was a spiritual teacher in ancient India and the founder of Buddhism. His teachings form the foundation of the Buddhist religion.

Slash-and-Burn Farming: An agricultural technique where land is cleared by cutting and burning vegetation. It enriches the soil temporarily but can lead to deforestation and soil erosion.

Soorphanaka: Demoness sister of the Demon King Tosakan, analogous to Ravana's sister in the Indian Ramayana. Known for her fierce nature.

Sukhothai Kingdom: The first independent Thai kingdom founded in 1238, known as the "Dawn of Happiness." It was a period noted for the development of Thai art, architecture, and the establishment of Theravada Buddhism as the dominant religion.

Surasa: The divine Nagini or sea nymph from the Ramakien. She is the female giant snake creature involved in testing and challenging heroes, like Hanuman.

Theravada Buddhism: The oldest form of Buddhism, focusing on the teachings of the Buddha as preserved in the Pali Canon.

Threefold Training: In Buddhism, the threefold training is the teaching of ethical conduct, mental discipline, and wisdom.

Three Marks of Existence: In Buddhism, the three characteristics of all existence are impermanence, suffering, and nonself.

Tiryagyoni Realm: The realm of animals in Buddhist cosmology, characterized by ignorance and instinctual living.

Triple Gem: The three pillars of Buddhism: the Buddha (enlightened One), the Dharma (teachings), and the Sangha (monastic community).

Vanaras: Monkey-like beings in the Ramakien, akin to the Vanaras in the Ramayana, who assist Phra Ram.

Vinaya: The regulatory framework for the monastic community in Buddhism, detailing ethical conduct.

Vishnu: Vishnu, a major god in Hinduism, also known in Thailand as Phra Narai. He is revered for his role as the preserver and protector, often incarnated to restore cosmic order.

Vishwakarma: The divine architect of the gods in Hindu mythology, known for his prowess in crafting and building. He is credited with creating many of the gods' weapons and celestial abodes, utilizing his vast knowledge of architecture and engineering.

Wats: Monasteries in Thailand, serving as centers of Buddhist worship and community gatherings.

Yakshas: Natural spirits or deities, often depicted as spiritual guardians of places and treasures, often seen protecting temples in Thai and Khmer architecture. However, some can be considered mischievous or malicious.

Yants: Sacred geomantic designs in Southeast Asian culture depicting animals, deities, and inscriptions for sacred tattoos or magical objects. They are believed to offer protection, strength and good luck.